The Radical Gospel

When Jesus Transforms Your Life

Jayson Derowitsch

River Birch Press
Daphne, Alabama

The Radical Gospel
by Jayson Derowitsch
Copyright ©2020 Jayson Derowitsch

All rights reserved. This book is protected under the copyright laws of the United States of America. This book may not be copied or reprinted for commercial gain or profit.

Scripture is taken from the ESV® Bible (The Holy Bible, English Standard Version®), copyright ©2001 by Crossway, a publishing ministry of Good News Publishers. Used by permission. All rights reserved.

ISBN 978-1-951561-57-4 (Print)
      978-1-951561-58-1 (E-book)

For Worldwide Distribution
Printed in the U.S.A.

River Birch Press
P.O. Box 868, Daphne, AL 36526

Contents

Introduction   *v*

1   The True Problem of Humanity   *1*

2   Righteous Judge, Loving Creator   *8*

3   Sin, the Centric Disorder   *22*

4   The Radical Gospel   *34*

5   The Radical Gospel, Continued   *52*

6   A Testimony of Transformation   *68*

7   A Testimony of Happiness and Ministry   *82*

8   A Testimony of Enduring through Tragedy   *93*

9   Pain Becomes a Reason for Joy   *114*

10   Illogical Man, Illogical God?   *125*

11   How to Discern Truth through the Mysteries of God   *148*

12   Stand Firm and Endure in Obedience   *175*

13   A Proverbial Future   *189*

Introduction

The Radical Gospel—what do you think when you read those words? Some may have a history of disappointment, where the gospel has become no more than a catchphrase. Others may have confusion toward what the gospel even is. Yet others may have a full understanding of the gospel. One thing I've discovered is that there is no person I know who does not want to be radically changed for the better.

The gospel of Jesus Christ is a life-altering and life-transforming phenomenon. It's good news! However, many people I know personally have attempted to experience the gospel and felt little to no result as an outcome. Much of the world has become skeptical toward the legitimacy of the gospel because with every great testimony, there is another testimony of indifference and disappointment. I fear the gospel appears to many as a great attempt at "make-believe."

In my estimation, there are a few reasons why a person may have trouble experiencing the gospel. First, they may not have a sufficient understanding of why we even need the gospel, what the gospel is, and what it really does. Second, they may have trouble truly committing their whole life to God. Third, they may give up because the world hits back hard. When these things take place, it results in what I call a "feigned spirituality"—that is, earnestly believing in a spiritual process when the believed process isn't actually the gospel. This, of course, leads to major disappointment and distrust in the good news whose life-altering reality has been testified about by so many others.

I empathize with anyone who has experienced such disappointment, because I was that person, as well. I tried the gospel, and it didn't work! I didn't feel any change. I didn't see an immediate improvement in my life. However, I was also too stubborn to give up. I spent years attempting to know God and experience His gospel through study, tradition, practice, and many other methods.

I finally experienced the gospel in a rather miraculous way—and I have been experiencing it change my life for the last fifteen years. I discovered what I had missed and also what I had to give in order to truly have a relationship with Jesus Christ that was ever-growing and consistently changing me. I lacked understanding and commitment. I have certainly had my share of the world knocking me down, but once I met Jesus personally, it made all the difference.

I want this experience for everyone. If you have been that person who has doubted the gospel, or given up on it, then these next chapters are for you. What I have to share is the knowledge and experience I've gone through that has resulted in a radical gospel change in my life. This experience is not set aside for certain people. God says clearly that He wants all to be saved and experience the truth (1 Tim. 2:4-6).

The Radical Gospel of Jesus Christ is the biggest life change you will ever experience, if you really choose to experience it God's way. Are you ready to see what that looks like?

1

The True Problem of Humanity

Vanity of vanities, says the Preacher, vanity of vanities! All is vanity. What does man gain by all the toil at which he toils under the sun? A generation goes, and a generation comes, but the earth remains forever (Eccl. 1:1–3).

The author declares, "Vanity of vanities! All is vanity." This is the conclusion of arguably the wisest man to ever live, King Solomon. According to this rather somber book, Ecclesiastes, the king observes life and realizes that there is a commonality with all people: We all die! So, why does it matter one iota how we conduct ourselves in this world if the end is the same? We work and toil for the vapor of life that we have, but at the end of the road, if our end is the same as everyone else's, we might as well "eat, drink, and be merry."

I'll never forget my childhood dreams. I suppose they aren't so very different from any other boy's dreams. I longed for that awesome Corvette to drive. I imagined playing professional basketball while also being a kung-fu master. I dwelled on the idea of traveling the world and seeing everything this earth has to offer. I delighted in the thought of eating the best foods from every culture. Of course, I couldn't do all these things and not have the biggest mansion anyone has ever seen. All of these desires were happiness at face value. The dream was that once they happened, I would experience happiness like I hadn't before. I'm not complaining here. Dreaming like this certainly isn't the worst way to spend those childhood years.

However, one thing I rarely thought about was death. It gave me the heebie-jeebies. When I did think of it, it was like a code red emergency, and my brain extended all efforts to get my mind away from that thought. Young people shouldn't have to think about death, right? Young people are invincible until they are at least thirty years old, or so I thought. Yet, this idea of death came back around from time to time, and I couldn't shake it. Why do people die? That's a good question for a young person. When I attempted to answer it, it almost always resulted in sadness and depression. It was then that I realized people spent so much effort trying to avoid thinking or talking about death because there are no good feelings at the end of that stream.

I believe my childhood dreams were all focused on how to achieve my happiness because the alternative felt terrible. Consequently, many people strive for material things to fill the void of their happiness, which leads to another great question—what brings happiness? Pondering these questions as a youth led me to have an appreciation for the book of Ecclesiastes.

It is no small thing that Ecclesiastes was authored by Solomon. His history makes the message quite the conundrum. Fathom for a moment the man who had everything of value, as we tend to measure value. He had seven hundred wives and three hundred concubines. He literally had a thousand women available to him for whatever reason whenever he asked. Tradition says that he had the most extensive

The True Problem of Humanity

supply of gold and precious metals ever compiled in the history of mankind up to that point. It was not uncommon for foreign kings to send shiploads of gold as gifts to the king. His kingdom extended from the border of Egypt to the Euphrates River. During his time, all other kingdoms were subject to him; and if he decided, he potentially could have taken over the known world via military campaign or a diplomatic vassal treaty. Beyond this, he had been given the supernatural ability to gain wisdom from God Himself. So, to recap, we have the man who had all the women, money, power, and wisdom he could ever want or ask for, and what was his message to the world? All is vanity, a vapor that ends the same for everyone: in death!

Now, obviously this is an archaic, old-world message that has no applicable nature to our world today, right? I mean, it's not like sex, money, and power are prime motivators to humans in our own culture. It's not like people are striving to get educated so they can apply their knowledge and wisdom to benefit themselves and the people around them. The twenty-first-century human being has reached the pinnacle of sophistication and does not bother himself with the ways of old-world barbarity.

The irony is that one only has to glimpse at the United States of America to see the book of Ecclesiastes played out like a fiddle. If people aren't seeking power through the medium of politics or big business, then they are seeking wealth through the stock market or other investments. Those who don't pursue a college education to gain knowledge and understanding are most likely seeking fame through sex, drugs, rock and roll, sports, media, or other avenues. And for those who fall through the cracks, who don't leap into any one pursuit, we call these the lazy bums of society. They aren't interested in fame, or work, or power. They are, in fact, the truly smart ones, for they realize that they can live with a full stomach, entertainment, and shelter.

They eat, drink, and are merry, all on the backs of those who work and pay for their meal ticket. But who are the real schmucks here? If the message of Solomon has any validity to our lives today, then those who realize that a vapor is all they have will fill that time with pleasure and happiness, for in the end they will be in the same place as all the others.

Another question that must be asked is whether or not people realize the depressing reality of death. Why would people keep striving forward if they know that every effort will end in loss? Well, the massive explosion of anti-anxiety and anti-depression drugs in our world would suggest that people are fully aware of it, but they don't want to face that reality. They want to be numbed and blissfully ignorant, thinking that their fate will somehow be different from all those who have preceded them. Therefore, they flood their spare time with all sorts of entertainment that pleases the senses, such as media, food, music, or games. They give themselves no time to sit and think, for when they do they often need to pop a Prozac down their throats.

The reality of our modern society is Ecclesiastical. We are no different than Solomon, but most of us could never hope to match the level of wealth, power, and fame he achieved. Yet he still says that "all is vanity." Why should we think that our reality would be any different?

Solomon goes on to say, "And I applied my heart to seek and to search out by wisdom all that is done under heaven. It is an unhappy business that God has given to the children of man to be busy with" (Eccl. 1:13). Now, think for a moment of the work that men and women have had to apply themselves to, even in the last fifty years. Does not a vast majority of it revolve around death? Police exist to prevent people from killing or harming each other. Medical employees exist to prevent death, prolong life, slow decay, and improve quality of life, but ultimately, they have a 100 percent failure rate. Arts and entertainment exist ultimately to distract us from the reality of our own frailty. The production of goods exists primarily to sustain people in living as long as possible. Counselors attempt to help people think, feel, and process the reality of the hopelessness of death. It truly is an unhappy business that man has been busy with.

In contrast to this, think about the job sector if pain and death were not our reality. There would be no need for doctors, most counselors, and most police officers, and our entertainment would take a new form. There would be no need for food, or money, or the military if no one could die. Most of our needs would no longer exist, for there would be no sorrow awaiting us at the end of the road. Alas, this isn't our reality, and what we see in the form of hedonism is modern man's attempt to escape the depression of reality through drugs, alcohol, entertainment, and pleasure. Just like Solomon, we still, to this day, eat, drink, and are merry.

Wisdom and knowledge must be the answer, then, correct? Money, wealth, power, and influence may be what drives the whole system forward, but it is truly wisdom and knowledge that provides the innovation for change. Solomon's response to this is:

Then I saw that there is more gain in wisdom than in folly, as there is more gain in light than in darkness. The wise person has his eyes in his head, but the fool walks in darkness. And yet I perceived that the same event happens to all of them. Then I said in my heart, "What happens to the fool will happen to me also. Why then have I been so very wise?" And I said in my heart that this also is vanity. For of the wise as of the fool there is no enduring remembrance, seeing that in the days to come all will have been long forgotten. How the wise dies just like the fool! (Eccl. 2:13–16).

Yes! Wisdom may have its place, and it is truly a far more noble pursuit than foolishness, but the end result is still the same. Vanity and vapor! False hope and swift decline! Death is the great equalizer, and it cares not about your stature. It takes freely from us all with no partiality. So, what hope do we have left? Perhaps we should eat, drink, and be blissfully and ignorantly merry.

However, Solomon ended his depression-laden rant with an epiphany of magnanimous proportion. He said:

The end of the matter; all has been heard. Fear God and keep his commandments, for this is the whole duty of man. For God will bring every deed into judgment, with every secret thing, whether good or evil (Eccl. 12:13–14).

It was this verse that propelled me as a young man toward understanding that there is a far bigger picture than what I see in this world. Though the distractions may be blissful, and the dreams may be fun, death is no longer something to avoid thinking about when it is not the end. Sometimes death is the very subject that opens our eyes to realities beyond what is at face value.

God, according to the wisest man who ever lived, is a game changer. It may just be that the business of man does not have to be all unhappy. For in this concept, "Fear God and keep His commandments," there echoes a theme of justice and righteousness. Where there is a judgment, death cannot be the end of things. Death may be our universal problem, but there is hope! However, a decision must be made. If you decide that God is an archaic myth, then I suppose the remaining best option for you is this hedonism we so presently enjoy. I am confident that man is neither smart enough nor powerful enough to change the common outcome of death. So, to you who choose not to believe, I say, have a vapor's worth of fun.

But to the one who chooses to believe that this God may indeed exist and who chooses to seek Him out, I say, perhaps we need to find out a little more about this God.

2

Righteous Judge, Loving Creator

I remember my younger years in church trying my best to understand the faith to which my parents seemed so devoted. It was difficult! First, you've got this 1,700-page book, which is supposedly the guidebook to life, and then multiple people are repeating truths from that book that are all vitally important, to them at least. Whom do you listen to? Which one is safe? Do you have to read the entire Bible from cover to cover to sufficiently understand what it means to believe in God?

I struggled with these questions in my adolescent years, and I couldn't find good answers to them. It is assuredly for this reason that I never truly committed to God until I was in college. I searched out anyone who could help me, who could give me some nugget of wisdom, and I was left with discontentment. I determined that faith was a hard and complicated thing, and that it wasn't worth the time to pursue it. Due to my childlike complacency, I spent years missing out on the answer to the one big question that had eluded me.

Who Is God?

Most people I've come across in the present and the past have a high confidence in their knowledge of who God is, but in reality, they have more so fabricated a God who fits their personal bias rather than sought out the undeniable traits and actions of the God of Scripture. Therefore, I am often confronted by the hippie Jesus, or the militant Jesus, and, of course, the Santa Claus Jesus, but all of these biases greatly malign the Jesus of Scripture. These people have, in essence, taken a knife and cut out every bit of Scripture that does not agree with their frail view of the infinite God.

Any challenge to the status quo leads to arrogant eye-rolling, and an appeal to their faith as an unchallengeable proof that their view is correct. This is the primary problem! This is where dissension begins! If we want to return to unity, then we must come to an agreement on who God is.

Having spent approximately fifteen years professionally studying Scripture, I have found the question "Who is God?" to be one of the most difficult to answer in an exhaustive manner. It is easy to describe God by one of His attributes. For example, "God is merciful" is a very true description, but not in all circumstances. Sometimes He is not merciful. To give a modern-day example, answer the question, Who is Paul McCartney? Some might say he is a Beatle. Others might say he is a musician. Still others might say he is an artist. Yet, Sir Paul might just look at those descriptions and say, "That's only one small facet of my life, for I am far more than just those things." If we have trouble adequately answering that question for a finite person, how can we adequately answer that question for an infinite God?

Therefore, in my attempt to answer this question, I will not be so bold as to profile God by using a contemporary worldview. Rather, my method is to simplify down to two descriptors so that, wherever we open the Bible, we can see present in the person of God these two elements, constantly and consistently. God is first a loving Creator, and second, a righteous Judge. No matter where you look in Scripture, I can guarantee that you will see both a loving Creator and a righteous Judge.

Toward the view of loving Creator, there are multiple evidences. First, we must take into account John's very blatant claim,

> *Beloved, let us love one another, for love is from God, and whoever loves has been born of God and knows God. Anyone who does not love does not know God, because God is love* (1 John 4:7–8).

In saying that God is love, John is saying that the very nature of God is love. There is something very organic and fundamentally present in the person of God that is so big and indescribable, we have to relegate it to the word "love." This is not to say that the human view of love is what dictates who God is, but rather that God shows humanity what love is.

Love has such a large semantic range, there is no telling how people choose to define it and subsequently associate their definition of love with God. In doing this, they damage and distort an accurate description of God with what they have made up according to their modern bias and worldview. Therefore, our presupposition should be that we have absolutely no clue what love is. Thankfully John gives us more.

> *In this the love of God was made manifest among us, that God sent his only Son into the world, so that we might live through him. In this is love, not that we have loved God but that he loved us and sent his Son to be the propitiation for our sins* (1 John 4:9–10).

The primary example of love given in Scripture is that God sent His only Son to be the propitiation for our sins, so that we might live through Him. In this act we see multiple actions and dispositions present. These include a deep caring for others, self-sacrifice, a desire for healing, and finally a desire for closeness. If we latch on to these things and incorporate them into our lives, then our understanding of love will grow exponentially.

Now, where does the Creator part fit into this? One need not look further than the beginning and the end: Genesis and Revelation. "In the beginning, God created the heavens and the earth" (Gen. 1:1). Why did He create the heavens and the earth?

> *Then God said, "Let us make man in our image, after our likeness. And let them have dominion over the fish of the sea and over the birds of the heavens and over the livestock and over all the earth and over every creeping thing that creeps on the earth" (Gen. 1:26).*

God made everything as a gift for His pinnacle of creation—man. It was all made for the creation constructed in His own image and likeness. In this creation, we see the qualities of love present, as well. We see a desire for closeness and relationship. We see a self-sacrificial giving, for none of this world was designed solely for Him. The only creation that God made that was designed strictly for Himself was mankind. Therefore, God gave to man much, with the only expected return being a worshipful relationship. What we see in the Genesis account is love and creation working in unison.

Now, fast-forward to the end of the story. The apostle John, in the book of Revelation, declares:

Then I saw a new heaven and a new earth, for the first heaven and the first earth had passed away, and the sea was no more. And I saw the holy city, New Jerusalem, coming down out of heaven from God, prepared as a bride adorned for her husband. And I heard a loud voice from the throne saying, "Behold, the dwelling place of God is with man. He will dwell with them, and they will be his people, and God himself will be with them as their God. He will wipe away every tear from their eyes, and death shall be no more, neither shall there be mourning, nor crying, nor pain anymore, for the former things have passed away." And he who was seated on the throne said, "Behold, I am making all things new...." (Rev. 21:1–5).

It is certainly not a coincidence that God, at the end of the story, does quite the same thing as He did at the beginning of the story. Primarily because He is a loving Creator, in His love not only has He created a new heavens and a new earth, but He has created a way for His people to enjoy it without pain, death, crying, or mourning. Once again, we see the fundamental elements of love—self-sacrifice, deep caring for others, a desire for healing, and a desire for closeness—and we see it further manifested through a vast creation. God is undeniably a loving Creator who is acting out His very nature through the whole story of Scripture.

He is also a righteous Judge. In declaring Him righteous, we must take into account the meaning of the word "righteous." In its essence, to be righteous is to be consistently right, suggesting that there is a definite corresponding wrongness. Therefore, God in His righteousness is not just always right, but He is also making all things right. Consider this passage:

> *The Lord judges the peoples; judge me, O Lord, according to my righteousness and according to the integrity that is in me. Oh, let the evil of the wicked come to an end, and may you establish the righteous—you who test the minds and hearts, O righteous God! My shield is with God, who saves the upright in heart. God is a righteous judge, and a God who feels indignation every day* (Ps. 7:8–11).

What we see here is that righteousness is the foundational fuel that powers judgment. "God is a righteous judge"! Therefore, we must understand that the judgment, whether harsh or not, is not primarily attacking people, but rather the wrong that is corresponding to them. It just so happens that people are inextricably linked to the wrong that they do. Furthermore, it is encouraging to know that righteousness and goodness go hand in hand. Consider these other two passages:

> *Far be it from you to do such a thing, to put the righteous to death with the wicked, so that the righteous fare as the wicked! Far be that from you! Shall not the Judge of all the earth do what is just?* (Gen. 18:25)

> *Even though you offer me your burnt offerings and grain offerings, I will not accept them; and the peace offerings of your fattened animals, I will not look upon them. Take*

away from me the noise of your songs; to the melody of your harps I will not listen. But let justice roll down like waters, and righteousness like an ever-flowing stream (Amos 5:22–24).

The Genesis passage reclarifies that God, indeed, being the Judge of all the earth, will be just or right. The Amos passage gives a very good image of how that plays out. God states that He will not accept burnt offerings, songs, or anything that leads into worship. Why? Are these not good things? Usually yes, they are, but in the context of the Israelites, they were worshiping other gods on the side, and God wasn't about to have any of that. So, He urged them to "let justice roll down like waters, and righteousness like an ever-flowing stream." In that statement, He gives both encouragement and a warning.

God is telling them to start doing what is right, and perhaps His judgment on the issue would change, but if they don't, justice and righteousness will still be done. Much like you can't stop water from moving, you just as well can't stop righteousness from happening. So, their punishment, their judgment, was to be exiled from their land. Goodness is a by-product of righteousness. Righteousness is the action, whereas goodness is the descriptor. Therefore, righteous people ought to be producing good things. When they don't, they usually have some sort of challenge from God to change their practices, as we can see in the Scriptures above.

Now, this loving Creator and righteous Judge makes perfect sense separately, right? Multiple examples of both exist throughout Scripture; we cannot deny that God judges, nor can we deny that He loves us. Yet people have proficiently attempted to separate these two. I think of statements like, "The God of the Old Testament was wrathful and judging, but the God of the New Testament is full of love, mercy, and grace." However, we must conclude that if God is both of these things all the time, then we must also be aware that when He judges, He judges in the context of His love and creativeness. For if we believe in a modal God who is different at different times, then we must ask, when is God not righteous? When is He not a judge? Or better yet, at what point does God cease to love? I believe that God is all of these things at the same time—always.

To back this idea up with Scripture, let us look at the precursor to the flood:

> *The Lord saw that the wickedness of man was great in the earth, and that every intention of the thoughts of his heart was only evil continually. And the Lord regretted that he had made man on the earth, and it grieved him to his heart. So the Lord said, "I will blot out man whom I have created from the face of the land, man and animals and creeping things and birds of the heavens, for I am sorry that I have made them* (Gen. 6:5–7).

I've heard it asked many times, "Why would a loving God flood the whole earth and kill all but a handful of humanity?" This is a great question, but most people tend to read past this Scripture, which explains why God had to flood the earth. So, what are the elements of the process here? If we indeed have a loving Creator and a righteous Judge, then we should see all of this in the flood account. So, how was the earth during this time? Every person was wicked, having only evil intentions in their hearts continually. Based on this, it should be easy to see why the righteousness and judgment of God had to be manifested on the earth. How could He allow such evil to prevail when there was nothing to counteract it? There was only one family who wasn't fully evil, and that was Noah's.

Now to the love of God. Where is that in this story? The next verse says, "The Lord regretted that he had made man on the earth, and it grieved him to his heart." There is no good commentary, nor an explanation from man, that I believe can adequately explain what "it grieved him to his heart" was really like. Since we can't comprehend it, I think we tend to overlook it. But the reality of God's love was such that even though all He was looking at was pure evil all the time, there was a sadness in Him, defying human comprehension, that His once-good creation, which had been made in His own image, had now chosen a defiled and wicked lifestyle. How could He kill His own children, whom He had designed to be part of His family? Yet how could He let evil and wickedness mock His righteousness?

This is where we see the tension that exists in the person of God the Father. Love dictates that grace and long-suffering are necessary to give humanity every possible chance to enter into righteousness. However, righteousness dictates that evil must be judged. So, how did God present this to the people of the earth prior to the flood?

From the time that God presented to Noah His plan to flood the world, there were multiple years before He actually did it. Some scholars would even suggest this time period as close to one hundred years. How do we know? Well, Noah and his sons didn't build that ark in a day. With many years of Noah building the ark in the midst of the world population, God showed His love through communicating the impending judgment that was to come upon them. Had the people of the world repented in that time, then the flood might not have happened. Yet after all those years, nothing had changed despite Noah's warning, and the righteous judgment of God did come upon the earth. In the flood account, we do see a loving Creator and a righteous Judge.

Let's consider another biblical account:

> *Then the Lord said, "I have surely seen the affliction of my people who are in Egypt and have heard their cry because of their taskmasters. I know their sufferings, and I have come down to deliver them out of the hand of the Egyptians and to bring them up out of that land to a good and broad land, a land flowing with milk and honey, to the place of the Canaanites, the Hittites, the Amorites, the Perizzites, the Hivites, and the Jebusites. And now, behold, the cry of the people of Israel has come to me, and I have also seen the oppression with which the Egyptians oppress them"* (Ex. 3:7–9).

This is the beginning of the Exodus, in which God commissioned Moses to go to Pharaoh as His representative. But what do we see in this text? "I have surely seen the affliction of my people who are in Egypt and have heard their cry.... I know their sufferings and I have come down to deliver them...." Is this not a loving God who is declaring that He will create a way for them to leave and then provide them with a new land? It seems very plain to see the love of God here, but what about the Egyptians? The natural assumption is that God had reserved His righteous judgment for the Egyptians, and in many respects, He did.

However, we can even see the love of God manifest in how He treated the Egyptians. He gave them ten plagues. He didn't have to, for in His righteousness He could have just wiped them out. Yet what He did was provide ten opportunities for the Egyptian people to realize that He had power over all their gods, and they could repent and follow Him. According to Scripture, quite a number of them did. Some would suggest that only a sadistic being would toy with the ones He intended to destroy. However, I believe there is enough evidence to suggest that God would have not judged them like He did had the Egyptians all repented and just let the Israelites go.

Finally, to give the best example of this combination of loving Creator and righteous Judge, one need look no further than the centric belief of the Christian faith: the death, burial, and resurrection of Christ.

Philippians 2:5–8 states:

> *Have this mind among yourselves, which is yours in Christ Jesus, who, though he was in the form of God, did not count equality with God a thing to be grasped, but emptied himself, by taking the form of a servant, being born in the likeness of men. And being found in human form, he humbled himself by becoming obedient to the point of death, even death on a cross.*

Fathom for a moment the God of everything, watching evil manifest in His own creation then spread like wildfire throughout all that is good. This righteous God must judge evil, or else He is not truly Righteous. However, He also loves the creation that He made, those whom He purposed for a relationship with Him. The tension between the love that is His very nature, and His righteousness that demands judgment, leaves Him in a quandary. How does He achieve both, without another worldwide destruction? Even better, how could He accomplish this without any mass destruction? Could God even do that?

What we see is that God did something counterintuitive. He (Jesus) gave up the glory of the Godhead and embraced the full weakness of human flesh. In this move, He willingly sacrificed His own life—a life now susceptible to sin (Rom. 8:3), yet He never partook of it. Instead, He immersed Himself into the world full of evil, remained pure, and in a masterful show of creativity, and love, and righteousness, and judgment, He died a sacrificial death, taking due judgment on Himself instead of the world and executing that judgment in death. What did that death provide?

Upon His death, Christ appeased the tension of the righteous judgment of God that was intended for the world. Upon His resurrection, Christ initiated a new creation available to all who wish to accept it. Consider this passage:

> *For the love of Christ controls us, because we have concluded this: that one has died for all, therefore all have died; and he died for all, that those who live might no longer live for themselves but for him who for their sake died and was raised. From now on, therefore, we regard no one according to the flesh. Even though we once regarded Christ according to the flesh, we regard him thus no longer. Therefore, if anyone is in Christ, he is a new*

creation. The old has passed away; behold, the new has come (2 Cor. 5:14-17).

This Scripture communicates that the value of Christ's death is culminated in everyone's death to the flesh. What this means is that all people who are in Christ, meaning they have accepted His sacrifice and chosen to believe in Him as their God, are no longer viewed by God as a creation of flesh, but of spirit instead. God looks past the flesh and sees His new creation of a righteous Spirit, infused and in union with the Holy Spirit.

In this context, the flesh becomes a meaningless thing. So meaningless, in fact, that God has a new model of physical body awaiting us upon our judgment at the end of the age. To the believer, death to the body should be of very little worry, since we have already died to the body, the flesh. Consequently, I don't believe God views death to the body as a major issue, either. He is primarily focused on the spirit, His new creation.

Nevertheless, this new creation would never have existed had God not satisfied every aspect of who He is in the process. His love was made manifest through Christ's leaving heaven and becoming incarnated into flesh (John 3:16). His creativity was made manifest through the blood covenant made through Christ's death. His righteousness was made manifest through the fact that Christ never sinned, but He was the pure and perfect sacrifice. Finally, His judgment was made manifest through Christ's suffering on the cross, and His death, which separated Him from the Father for a time. It was a sacrifice He did not deserve, but that He gave on behalf of the world.

This is the God whom people have all seen, but few regarded, for people want their militant Jesus, and their Santa Claus Jesus, and their hippie Jesus. Yet when we view the pinnacle of the redemptive plan of God, what we see is a loving Creator and a righteous Judge.

For those of you who have struggled with this question like I did as a young man, I will give you the honest truth. It took me many years of studying the Bible before I arrived at this conclusion with confidence. However, that does not mean I didn't gain a better understanding of God as I progressed, and the same can be true for you. Look at the Scriptures for yourself, and step by step, you will understand God better each and every day.

3

Sin, the Centric Disorder

Sin was the thing that made church almost unbearable while I was growing up. I found it so frustrating that people could so quickly condemn others for their sin when they were also sinful, but they hid it better. Some people would say that all sin was the same, while others would say there were worse sins than others. Yet most all would say that sin was an action. It was confusing! Why was it that a pastor, whose wife divorced him, had sufficiently ruined his career and life, when another leader who was pathologically lying to people got little more than a slap on the wrist? These sorts of things happened all the time, and as a young man, I saw it as a great form of hypocrisy.

However, I couldn't define sin any better than anyone else, so it was an inconvenience that I had to live with because who was I to challenge the status quo? Sin was certainly bad, but I didn't know much beyond that, so I kept my mouth shut. It wasn't until I was in Bible college that I truly began to see sin for what it really was—a disease!

Sin is the universal and centric disease that affects all of humanity. Talk about a pandemic. All pain, all suffering, all depression, sadness, and evil acts are a result of sin. It's not always the sin of the one experiencing the results of it, though all have sinned and fallen short of God's glory. Yet people

Sin, the Centric Disorder

have a strange way of defending their innocence. I think of phrases like, "But I'm a good person, why is this happening to me?" or, "It's not like I'm a serial killer." We like to compare our righteousness to others in order to feel better, and we like to think that our suppression of evil acts makes us better somehow.

I've got news for you: We all suffer from this nasty disease called sin, and sin leads to a serious case of deadness. The fact that we all will die proves that we all suffer from the sin disease. You, dear reader, may agree with my statement, but then you may say, "Okay, we all have sin, but that doesn't make me an evil person." My response would be, "Yes, it does."

Evil is merely the adjectival form of sin. Sin is a noun, a thing. Evil is what sin looks like when it manifests into something. Therefore, a little white lie is evil, and so is murder, and partiality, and greed, etc. In this context, everyone is evil to an extent. But again, we try so valiantly to downplay our own evils and spotlight all the evils of others. Why? If everyone suffers from sin and has a capacity for evil, then why try to hide it? What is there in this world that makes us so uneasy about our sin?

As was mentioned in the first chapter, the author of Ecclesiastes paints the picture so well. What prevents us from the practice of "eat, drink, and be merry," ignoring all the other horrific parts of life, is one simple truth: There is a God; God has a standard; and by His standard, He will judge the living and the dead. If you can believe there is a God, and you understand that God is loving, creative, righteous, and judging, then the very disease that has separated you from Him is the one that will be your downfall come judgment time, unless it is dealt with.

Now, this is where sin gets quite difficult. Most people who understand God and choose to believe in God, submitting to His lordship and becoming a true follower, will have their sin blotted out. They will experience redemption. They will become a new creation. However, a large number of people have bought the deception that their perceived goodness has capabilities leading to salvation.

Though they believe in God, they don't believe that the depravity of man is truly universal. Either that, or they don't believe that God's judgment is truly meant to eradicate sin. Or, the more clever approach, God does eradicate sin, but He separates the person from their sin, and the person eventually experiences salvation. What does this look like in our modern culture? A notable author has suggested, "Would God really send Gandhi to hell?" Would a loving God do that? And so this deception has played out. Good people shouldn't go to hell, says the wise modern man. Yet one fatal flaw permeates this line of thinking.

How do we, a fallen and sin-corrupted people, have any clue what "good" looks like? We throw this term around so flippantly and arrogantly, as if good is an easily known, understood, and witnessed activity. But ponder for a moment what is our actual reality. We live in a cursed earth, ravaged by a worldwide flood sent to eradicate wicked people. Yet we call many parts of this earth beautiful. We grow up watching people slowly decay until their bodies stop working and they die. If this happens after their eightieth birthday, we tend to think of it as normal. If it happens before old age, we say, "What a shame." If it happens to a kid, we question God's goodness. We selfishly desire money, possessions, and fame, and we call these things inherently good because it's been universally accepted for so long.

Sin, the Centric Disorder

The point being, like a goldfish that lives in a twenty-gallon tank, if we all have grown up only knowing a sin-corrupted life, then how can we truly recognize what is really good? I've heard believers say, "This earth is so beautiful and magnificent," when, in reality, God finds much of it ugly. If He didn't, He wouldn't be planning to dispose of it and make a new one. We are caught in our twenty-gallon tank, thinking we have sufficient knowledge of the entire ocean. We think death is normal because everyone dies, yet God says, "For he must reign until he has put all his enemies under his feet. The last enemy to be destroyed is death" (1 Cor. 15:25–26).

If death is an enemy of God, then why do we act like it is just a part of life? We grow up in the context of death, and we train our minds and beliefs to say that certain types of death are abhorrent, but other types of death are normal. If that is our rationale, then I dare say we are so far removed from "good" and "life" that our only other option for a moral compass is, as Francis Schaeffer penned, the "moving consensus of men." I don't know about you, but I would rather not have morally ignorant people be the arbiters of right and wrong for the culture in which I live.

Thankfully, we have the Bible as our guide, right? Yet how can someone corrupted by the disease of sin comprehend the truth of Scripture without corrupting the truth they have received? Indeed, have we not seen this in abundance? We now have the social justice gospel, biblical feminists, patriarchal hierarchists, the Jesus Movement, biblical higher criticism, the initial evidence of tongues, entire sanctification, the Emergent Church movement, and theistic evolution, and if I kept the list going, I could easily fill up two full pages of movements, methods, or doctrines that have recklessly distorted Scripture. We've all done it to some extent, but only a few can see their folly and humbly return to the acceptance that we know far less than we think we know. Sin is the culprit in all of this.

If you haven't guessed it yet, sin distorts everything. It breaks down, it destroys, and it wreaks havoc in every aspect of people's lives. On the other hand, it is elusive. It hides well. So well, in fact, that the only evidence we have of sin that no one can deny is pain and death, and the world has come to the conclusion that death is ordinary. So, sin remains diminished from view.

Yes! The abstract view of sin dominates our culture today. The average person has a very basic concept of sin, considering it an essence that is bad or evil, but finding no way to define it in tangible and practical terms. Therefore, we shift sin, right along with the moral standards decided by an ever-changing majority of human beings.

A prime example of this would be a look at homosexuality over the last one hundred years in America. In 1918, a gay person would be anathema in society. The overwhelming majority of people would view homosexual behavior as a wrong or sinful thing. Yet through many social movements, and protests, and political actions, we fast-forward to 2020. In our modern day, a homosexual lifestyle is considered a perfectly fine practice. In fact, the overwhelming majority of people now find the deep-rooted wrongness to lie in those people who still maintain that being gay is wrong.

In one hundred years, we have seen a complete reversal of what sin looks like on a particular issue. This is what the "moving consensus of men" looks like. Because of this, we now have a major problem. What is sin?! Was the 1918 view correct, or is the 2020 view correct? Or are both a little bit

Sin, the Centric Disorder

wrong, and sin is really a viewpoint that hasn't been seen yet? Furthermore, who gets to decide what the correct view of sin is? Should it truly be a majority-based thing?

Perhaps a social and scientific experiment is in order here. I suggest that the vast majority of people publicly declare that we are no longer sinful beings. I would think that many would welcome that notion. So, make the declaration that humans are no longer sinful beings and that none of our actions are sinful, and then see if we still die. In that case, if we still die, then there is the proof that our majority consensus has absolutely no influence on what sin actually is. For the Bible states, "The wages of sin is death…" (Rom. 6:23). So, if we still die, then the Bible is correct in its statement, and we have no power to change that. Therefore, to say we can be the arbiters of defining sin seems foolish.

This means we must become interpreters of past history to discover what sin is. However, there are further problematic things to overcome. Which view of history is the correct view? From a religious perspective alone, we have Hinduistic history, Buddhist history, Judeo/Christian history, Islamic history, Daoist history, and the list goes on.

Compound that with secular history, and we have Greek, Roman, Hittite, Persian, Babylonian, Egyptian, and Assyrian narratives perpetuated due to their status as major empires. So, which history is the one that really defines sin? Will we find it in Greek culture, or Hindu culture, or perhaps Egyptian culture? Who knows? This is the primary problem in an unbelieving world. We can't deny that evil exists, and that sin in some capacity is real, but we also can't determine the root of what sin is.

Once we determine which history is the correct narrative

to follow, then there is one more mountainous hurdle to overcome. How much of this history is actually real, and how much is fictitious or embellished to communicate a lesson? Why is this important? In essence, I can learn very useful moral lessons from the stories of the Greek gods, but knowing that they are not real, I do not have any historical tie-in upon which to base my belief. Rather, I have a moral proposition that I could either take or leave, and it really wouldn't have a space-time effect on me, apart from how other people react.

Therefore, if we want to discover the definition of sin in a satisfactory way, we must first discover these things: a space-time history that is accurate; a metanarrative that provides ample teaching on the subject; and a reality that goes beyond the sin-filled natural world—it must be supernaturally given. In using the term "metanarrative," what is meant is an all-encompassing story that explains the key philosophical life questions like, "Where did I come from?" and "What is my purpose?" It's a story that explains life.

The reason these three criteria are necessary is because each helps to validate the others' realness and truthfulness. For example, a metanarrative that is written throughout the context of space and time history helps to show that the story is actually real. Likewise, the supernatural origin of such a metanarrative gives legitimacy to a deity who is indeed involved in all of this.

Upon studying many different religions, whether monotheistic or polytheistic, I have found that most every one gives a compelling case in at least one of the three criteria mentioned above. Hinduism has many writings that are life-encompassing. Yet it lacks a definitive space-time history

Sin, the Centric Disorder

where there is a tie between humanity and deity. Contrasting this are the pantheons of the ancient empires, which had multiple real events in history that were considered a consequence of the gods' moods. What they lacked was a true, all-encompassing metanarrative that was universal. For both of these, it would be difficult to prove whether anything they believed was supernaturally given to them. Likewise, most other belief systems are in that same boat.

Is there a belief system out there that meets all of the criteria? The answer is yes, there are two. A Judeo-Christian belief is one of them, and an Islamic belief is the other. Both of these belief systems have a detailed metanarrative; they have a long historical line of space-time events that help make up their beliefs, but the Bible can be seen to be supernaturally given and the Quran largely borrows much of its content from the Bible. It is important to note that both, being monotheistic, share much of the same history because one book took much of its information from the other. So, what is the difference between the two? Many things, but to keep this simple, one major difference is historical.

The Jewish nation can date the time of the writing of their metanarrative beginning around 1400 BC. The Old Testament writings were completed prior to the time of Christ. All of the New Testament was written prior to 100 AD, and the Bible as we know it was fully compiled into one book by 400 AD. In contrast to this, the Islamic metanarrative (the Quran) wasn't even started until 609 AD by Muhammad, and he finished it within twenty-three years, in the year 632 AD. Considering the timeline, one could say that Muhammad owes a lot of credit to the Bible for his own work, since they do share a large portion of the same history.

But ultimately, content aside, each of these metanarratives must be viewed as legitimate to the time and history they talk about.

Where the Bible and the Quran differ greatly is that the Bible was largely written during or closely after the history it talks about, whereas the Quran was written far after the history it references. Therefore, which should be considered the more accurate text? Also, it is important to note that the Bible, being written over the span of 1,500 years, had at least forty authors contributing to it. Thus, its cohesiveness is supernatural. Nowhere else in history do we see such a cohesive story being written by as many authors over such a long period of time. The Quran pales in comparison, being written by one author over the span of twenty-three years. Nevertheless, due to such rich history, it should be no coincidence that proponents of Judeo-Christianity and Islam combined make up a quarter of the world population.

Therefore, by the three criteria and then the comparison of the metanarratives, it is my conclusion that the Bible provides the best chance for a full understanding of what sin is and how we relate to it. Nothing else comes remotely close to the Bible's history and accuracy. I say this with the full realization that I have not addressed many of the other religions present today. However, if we use these three criteria on any of them, what we will find is that all of them are deficient in at least one area, except for the Bible.

So, if the Bible ought to be our source for understanding sin, and answering all of our other philosophical questions, then what does it say about sin? Consider this passage:

Sin, the Centric Disorder

For the wrath of God is revealed from heaven against all ungodliness and unrighteousness of men, who by their unrighteousness suppress the truth. For what can be known about God is plain to them, because God has shown it to them. For his invisible attributes, namely, his eternal power and divine nature, have been clearly perceived, ever since the creation of the world, in the things that have been made. So they are without excuse. For although they knew God, they did not honor him as God or give thanks to him, but they became futile in their thinking, and their foolish hearts were darkened. Claiming to be wise, they became fools, and exchanged the glory of the immortal God for images resembling mortal man and birds and animals and creeping things. Therefore God gave them up in the lusts of their hearts to impurity, to the dishonoring of their bodies among themselves, because they exchanged the truth about God for a lie and worshiped and served the creature rather than the Creator, who is blessed forever! Amen (Rom. 1:18–25).

Though a definition and description of sin can be exhaustively applied to various situations and acts, in essence, this passage from Romans gives us the foundation of sin. Let us follow the train of thought:

1. The primary act of an unrighteous and ungodly person is the suppression of truth.
Why is this important?

2. Even though every person, in viewing the immense detail, diversity, and functionality of this earth, has developed an un-

derstanding of a Creator God in their hearts, they have rejected that truth and chosen to worship created things made by God or humans.

What is the result of this?

3. God let them continue down the path that they chose, which resulted in futile thinking, darkened hearts, and an arrogance of self-proclaimed wisdom, which ultimately dishonors their own bodies. Their bodies are worshiping something they were never created to worship.

This is sin! The suppression of truth that leads to people's rejection of God, culminating in a worship of something other than God.

This is how sin starts. It is a process of choice that results in a corrupt and dead spirit. That corrupt and dead spirit then results in a corrupt and dying flesh. The sin that first affects the spirit will ultimately affect the flesh.

The first two people made this choice, which subsequently affected all the rest of mankind from birth. We are born into that sin corruptness. We are born physically dying and spiritually dead. Furthermore, our practice in life is first to sin and then to dwell in sin. Sin lies to us, saying that we can dwell in it and experience life. If we don't recognize God, there is no hope for any type of real life apart from Him. Sin corrupts everything and masks the truth from us.

We can see the lie of sin develop over time. At first, the suppression of truth and rejection of God, being seen in the first major civilizations, was to believe that there were actually many different gods—a pantheon. Please notice that this lie didn't outright reject the notion of God. People still believed in the idea of supernatural deities. It didn't even reject all of the good truths revealed by God. It was really a slight change, but it was enough to deter the rightful worship toward the real God. Fast-forward to today, and what we see is the full and outright rejection of the existence of God.

God has become a myth in many peoples' minds and hearts because they have been saturated with thousands of years of lies and deceptions. Every scholarly and intellectual stream has found a foundation in devaluing and disproving God. Whether it's science, math, philosophy, literature, etc., what we are seeing is an ever-progressive march toward God becoming a foolish afterthought in the minds of humanity. This self-proclaimed wisdom of today is running rampant, and all who perpetuate this practice have been blinded to their own foolishness.

The older and wiser me truly wished that the younger me would have had a better grasp on what sin was and how it really worked within humanity. Without an understanding of sin that is sufficient, it is very difficult to know and understand why the gospel is so very important. The gospel is the answer to sin, and the young me couldn't believe in an answer to a problem I didn't know well. Now that sin and death have been thoroughly talked about, it is time to move forward to the good news!

4

The Radical Gospel

So, where is the good news in all of this?! If we have a world whose primary work revolves around the stark reality of death, and people live to make themselves ignorant to that reality; if we have an underlying reality of sin that fuels death, and it leads to us being sidetracked away from God; and if we know God to be a righteous Judge and also a loving Creator—then what is the solution to our plight? How can this awful cycle of sin and death be thwarted? How can we escape from this "eat, drink, and be merry" state of being, and experience something other than a feigned spirituality?

God has a plan! Things have happened that have brought about good news for the world. This is why we call it the gospel, or the *euangellion*—which literally means the "good news." Furthermore, it's not just any good news, but it's the radical good news. Radical means to "affect the fundamental nature of something." So, this good news isn't some trivial thing, but rather it is something that will change the essence of life and our current state as we know it.

What is the good news? Herein lies another problem in our world. The common, most popular thing to define the good news is to say that Jesus came, died, and rose again, thus atoning for our sins. All of this is very true, but it doesn't give the full picture, and it doesn't explain how any of it works.

Therefore, let's divide up what this good news entails and exactly how it can work in our lives.

Six components make up the gospel as depicted in Scripture: 1) God has established a kingdom; 2) God has made legal provision for us; 3) we are going to be re-created; 4) we can have a family relationship with God; 5) evil will be dealt with; and 6) we choose when we die. These components all combine to make this good news that God wants us to know, but we must delve deeply into each one to gain an appreciation for the full gospel.

1. God established a kingdom.

When Jesus began to preach, He didn't start His mission by saying, "I'm here to save the world from sin," or "I've come to defeat death once and for all." These are true statements, but they were not His primary purpose. The first thing Jesus said when He started His ministry was, "Repent, for the kingdom of heaven is at hand" (Matt. 3:2; see also Mark 1:15).

For all the focus we put on salvation, sanctification, atonement, love, mercy, and grace, believers certainly fall painfully short on viewing their existence as part of a kingdom. But why is the establishment of a kingdom good news?

Look back to the beginning. What was God's intent in creation? Did He create man to have dominion over the earth, living forever in a state of true innocence? Was His plan to have a centric relationship with mankind as human beings continued to develop underneath His sovereignty? The answer is yes to both of these questions—but sin ruined that plan. The fall of man effectively ripped apart what God was trying to do. No longer did He have a sovereign, benevolent kingdom over righteous people. He now had a cursed earth, and a people who had to be kicked out of the land He ruled to find a way on their own.

The rulership of the world was now firmly up in the air. Mankind had various different directions in which they could go, and all but one were terrible. What we see play out in the early chapters of Genesis (which spanned about 1,500 years) is a righteous lineage of people with whom God communicated, while the rest of the world sought its leadership and governance elsewhere. This is what led up to the flood account. When people sought rulership apart from God, the end result was that pure evil permeated the world all the time. The lack of a God-centric kingdom produced that!

Therefore, we could view the entire story of Scripture as one big master plan to restore the original kingdom that God had established. He started with a righteous line, but then the flood came and wiped out almost all of the world's population. After that time, only ten generations had come and gone before God chose Abram out of the land of Ur to form what would become the nation of Israel. No longer was there simply a genealogical tie between God's people; now a nation was officially being developed.

By the time the days of Moses rolled around, the nation of Israel was truly large enough to be a nation, and they needed laws to be governed by. After they exited Egypt, God gave them a law that would produce the type of characteristics found in godly people. Furthermore, He would be their true Leader in a theocracy, though He used people like Moses, Aaron, Joshua, and the judges to represent Him to the Israelites. There was only one hitch in this whole plan, and it was one that God knew all too well. Sin still existed within people. Romans 8:3 says that Jesus "condemned sin in the flesh." Prior to Jesus' work, sin ran rampant throughout the whole human construct. Therefore, God's law had to be rigid—even to the point of being draconian.

If the track record of humanity was that given enough time and left to their own whims, they would choose evil in abundance, it makes perfect sense that God had to be staunch with His law so that the people would not fall away. I believe this explains why the death penalty was so common in Old Testament Jewish law. This is reflected well in the book of Deuteronomy (the Second Law), in which we see the phrase, "You shall purge the evil from your midst" repeated many times. God certainly didn't want a déjà vu experience with the characteristics of the pre-flood civilization weaseling their way back into His people.

This was the modus operandi all throughout the times of the judges. God ruled, and He called out people to represent Him when Israel strayed too far away from Him or when other nations tried to influence or affect His people. Ironically enough, the most peace Israel experienced as a nation happened during the 430-year timespan of the judges. God's earthly system never worked better than that time. But there was a fundamental problem that hadn't yet been solved. All the people of the earth, whether Jewish or not, were still infected by this nasty thing called sin. However great God's laws were, they weren't going to change the construct of man.

What we see next is the sinfulness of humanity once again slowly take over. The Jews decided they wanted a king, a situation that started off relatively well, but then it quickly went south. God soon had to use the other nations to temporarily destroy their cities and scatter them across the earth. Upon their eventual return to their homeland, the Jews never really got their nation back, but their laws and their religious practices remained. The plan of God was moving forward without hindrance.

Eventually Rome came to power over the entire known world, including the land of Israel, and with it came all forms of immorality. In this context, God brought about the true magnum opus of His plan to restore His kingdom. Jesus became a human being, inserted Himself into a corrupt worldly government, and made the official announcement that He was bringing about a new kingdom. The first thing He was calling everyone to do was to repent.

Upon Jesus' arrival and the announcement of this new kingdom, the Jews thought that meant He was going to overthrow Rome. That would be the sign of the Messiah, or so they thought. However, Jesus' mission was much more focused. His kingdom had to accomplish one thing with absolute sufficiency: the eradication of sin. Whatever governmental system He developed could not be created within the context of sin. This was a vital component to God's plan because without sin being dealt with, the whole world would turn to evil once again, if given enough time.

Therefore, God developed a new kind of citizen—a spiritual citizen. Another way to say it is that those who have declared allegiance to God and surrendered their lives to Him now have citizen status in heaven. On earth, the flesh of a person is still subject to earthly kingdoms and governments, but the spirit of a person is not. The apostle Paul had the audacity to say things like,

The Radical Gospel

For to me to live is Christ and to die is gain. If I am to live in the flesh that means fruitful labor for me yet which I shall choose I cannot tell. I am hard pressed between the two. My desire is to depart and be with Christ, for that is far better. But to remain in the flesh is more necessary on your account (Phil. 1:21–24).

Paul fully understood the difference between the citizens of heaven and those of the earth. He knew the immense improvement that citizenry in heaven brought to the table. Like any normal person, he wanted to experience it in its entirety as soon as possible. Yet he was willing to stay behind in his current state for the benefit of others who didn't yet see what he could see. Now, if Paul was longing to be in heaven, and all that implied, we must ask the question, What is involved with citizenship in heaven?

The first and obvious component to citizenship in heaven is status. It's really not much different from what we see in our world today. Different people have different status levels in a country, whether it's immigrant status, refugee status, full national citizenship status, etc. Everyone has a status of some sort. With this status comes certain rights and privileges. Citizenship in God's kingdom carries the status of a family member and provides for these rights and privileges: salvation from sin, unhindered communication with God, peace that surpasses understanding that will guard your life, the hope of a future improved glory, perfect righteousness and justice, rewards for service, the ability to earn treasure that can't get stolen or taken, a prepared place for us by Jesus, and of course, eternal life.

Sounds pretty good, right? One thing this citizenry does

not have is corruption. It is perfect, and it functions without flaw or fault. The good news of God is that we have the opportunity to join this kingdom and nation of people who will live harmoniously together forever, with perfect morality and character. It is utopia to the highest degree. Part of God's gospel plan is to fully fix the world's government systems by implementing His own. His theocracy shall return!

In our current state, we see fallenness in every capacity of life, including our kingdoms, governments, and political systems. It should be no surprise that when the term government is used, oftentimes the first word that comes to our minds is corrupt. It makes it difficult to see how any government system on earth could be good. But when the believer takes on heavenly citizenship, that should be the primary focus of their life. The apostle Paul exemplifies this when he says, "Let every person be subject to the governing authorities. For there is no authority except from God, and those that exist have been instituted [appointed] by God" (Rom. 13:1).

It is worthy of note that Paul wrote these words during the reign of Emperor Nero—you know, the man who lit Rome on fire, blamed it on the Christians, and subsequently burned Christians alive in the streets as candles to light the city at night. Likewise, this is the same government who oversaw Paul's execution by beheading. If you think our government is bad, try comparing it to the Roman empire.

Regardless of how bad things get here, a citizen of heaven should be focused first and foremost on heaven and his or her status there. Nothing can take that away. People can kill the body (the flesh), but they can't kill the spirit, and they can't take away a believer's status as citizen of heaven. That is excellent news!

2. God has made legal provision for us.

Remember, God is a righteous judge! He is also orderly. Nothing in the story of Scripture manifests itself as something haphazard. Rather, God is a planner. He weighs the cost of whatever He does. Yet He is also a risk taker! His risks are structured in a system. That's simply the way He works, as we see in Scripture.

When the fall of man happened, the human race was bombarded with sin, which results in death. One question I often hear from people today is why God would allow that to happen in the first place. Why would a righteous and loving God create a system in which sin could even exist? The answer is that He is a risk taker—and He didn't want to have a relationship with robots.

Think about it for a second. How would you feel if you came home to your spouse and nothing happened until you came over and hit the kiss button? If only then would he or she come over and give you a kiss? No action would happen until you dictated it. Your spouse would only do what you ordered him or her to do. That would be awful! Part of the reason that our relationships are so unique and exciting is the fact that another person, who could reject you, has decided instead to accept you and be close to you.

Free will makes all the difference in the world when talking about relationships. God is a risk taker who wanted to create people who would truly choose Him. But in order to do that, He had to give them the option to reject Him. As the story turns out, those people did reject Him, but He still was not willing to give up on His creation. He implemented a system to create another chance for people to accept Him.

This is what I like to call the legal system of God. We see

various legal contracts throughout Scripture that help to give us a picture of how God's plan equates to our salvation. These contracts are called "covenants" in Scripture, but they are nevertheless legal and binding agreements.

The first legal thing we see God do in Scripture in regard to salvation is to cover Adam and Eve with animal skins. This might be easy to miss when reading through the story, but think about the implications: Adam and Eve were naked, which equated to shame after they sinned. God prepared animal skins to cover them, which presupposes that an animal had to die. What we have here is the first sacrificial atonement for sins. Blood was shed, and sins were covered. The wrath of God was appeased.

This sacrificial system was set up in the beginning and continued throughout Scripture. We see virtually every major prominent figure in the Old Testament building altars and sacrificing animals to atone for sin. As time went on, the procedures and observances became more intricate. By the time Jesus came on the scene, the Jews celebrated various festivals throughout the year, which were all centered on the sacrifice of animals in order to atone for sin. As Hebrews 10:1–4 informs us,

> *For since the law has but a shadow of the good things to come instead of the true form of these realities, it can never, by the same sacrifices that are continually offered every year, make perfect those who draw near. Otherwise, would they not have ceased to be offered, since the worshipers having once been cleansed, would no longer have any consciousness of sins? But in these sacrifices there is a reminder of sins every year. For it is impossible for the blood of bulls and goats to take away sins.*

God's legal system in the Old Testament was not sufficient to solve the sin problem. It was only sufficient to slow the decay of moral mankind until the true solution was presented. However, the people of this world needed a pattern to look at so that they would understand the true solution when it finally came.

Galatians 3:19–24 explains this well when it says:

> *Why then the law? It was added because of transgressions, until the offspring should come to whom the promise had been made, and it was put in place through angels by an intermediary. Now an intermediary implies more than one, but God is one. Is the law then contrary to the promises of God? Certainly not! For if a law had been given that could give life, then righteousness would indeed be by the law.*
>
> *But the Scripture imprisoned everything under sin, so that the promise by faith in Jesus Christ might be given to those who believe. Now before faith came, we were held captive under the law, imprisoned until the coming faith would be revealed. So then, the law was our guardian until Christ came, in order that we might be justified by faith.*

Remembering what the pre-flood world was like, the Old Testament Law makes a ton of sense. God never intended it to be the ultimate fix to the world's problems, but He intended it to be a guardrail, so the people of the world would not completely turn back to evil as had happened before. The yearly reminders of sin via the festivals and sacrifices kept His people from falling over the edge of moral decline. None of the laws fixed their sin problems, but they did prepare them to recognize and accept the true solution (Jesus) when He finally came.

This is what's so remarkable about Jesus' death, burial, and resurrection. Jesus was crucified and died on the Passover (the first of the festivals), He was buried and placed in the tomb on the Feast of Unleavened Bread (the second festival), and He was resurrected on the Feast of the First Fruits (the third festival). His blood sacrifice symbolized God saving His people out of a sinful world, just like He saved His people out of Egypt. The structure of the gospel coincides with the legal structure of Israel. Furthermore, we see the next festival, Pentecost, initiate the next part of the gospel, which was the giving of the Holy Spirit.

With this legal system of the Law in mind, and the festivals that God instituted, one glaring thing still should color our view of the gospel. There are three more festivals that God required of Israel, but no corresponding events have happened yet in association with them. These are the fall festivals of Trumpets, the Day of Atonement, and the Feast of Tabernacles. If God's gospel message truly coincides with the Law He created and implemented, then we don't have a fully completed gospel here! Some of the good news hasn't happened yet! There will be a legal conclusion to all of this.

This is truly an important distinction to make. It is all too easy to think of the end times or even the book of Genesis as not being related to the gospel. In my various encounters with Christians and other religious leaders, I generally hear things like, "Revelation is too confusing to figure out... I'm going to simply focus on Jesus and the gospel. The end will all work out." The problem with this line of thinking is that the end of the story is still part of the gospel!

Likewise, the beginning of the story also prepares the way for the gospel. Both are vital and essential parts of our faith in Jesus. God's legal plan permeates the entire story of Scripture, and the gospel coincides with His legal plan. We cannot systematize it, compartmentalize it, or prioritize it. It's all important. It's all interwoven into the gospel message. Therefore, if we wish to follow the gospel, we must become content with the notion of a Jesus who saves, but also a Jesus who will come again to declare war and destroy evil. The legal system of God ends with evil being fully dealt with— and then a new beginning. Again, that is excellent news!

3. We are going to be re-created.

If you are curious like me, at this point you might wonder how this kingdom declaration and this legal system of God has an effect on us right now. What is the good news of the gospel in the present?

Sure, claiming allegiance to God and His kingdom does have legal implications, such as citizenry and being incorporated into the overarching plan of God. But it also has existential implications. How you exist in the present and the future radically changes when the gospel invades your life.

When Jesus spoke with Nicodemus in John 3, He brought forth a life-altering idea that Nicodemus tried to wrap his mind around. Let's take a look at their dialogue:

> *Now there was a man of the Pharisees named Nicodemus, a ruler of the Jews. This man came to Jesus by night and said to him, "Rabbi, we know that you are a teacher come from God, for no one can do these signs that you do unless God is with him." Jesus answered him, "Truly, truly, I say*

to you, unless one is born again he cannot see the kingdom of God." Nicodemus said to him, "How can a man be born when he is old? Can he enter a second time into his mother's womb and be born?" Jesus answered, "Truly, truly, I say to you, unless one is born of water and the Spirit, he cannot enter the kingdom of God. That which is born of the flesh is flesh, and that which is born of the Spirit is spirit" (John 3:1–6).

Jesus proclaimed to Nicodemus that he must be born again to enter the kingdom of God. Truthfully, I wouldn't begrudge Nicodemus for not fully understanding what was being said, but Jesus drove the point home, as it is of the utmost importance. A spiritual birth must take place within humanity. Sin must be dealt with—and this is God's way of doing it.

To describe it further, we must take a much deeper look into the process of salvation. There are three words presented in Scripture that are used to explain the bigger concept of salvation—justification, sanctification, and glorification. Justification is another legal term, describing a legal process before God. To be justified is to "be considered and declared righteous." Even though sin still exists within the body, before God, the contract has been signed and the proceeding is over; the justified person is officially reconciled with God.

We see this in Romans 5:

Therefore, since we have been justified by faith, we have peace with God through our Lord Jesus Christ. Through him we have also obtained access by faith into this grace in which we stand, and we rejoice in hope of the glory of

God. Not only that, but we rejoice in our sufferings, knowing that suffering produces endurance, and endurance produces character, and character produces hope, and hope does not put us to shame, because God's love has been poured into our hearts through the Holy Spirit who has been given to us. For while we were still weak, at the right time Christ died for the ungodly. For one will scarcely die for a righteous person—though perhaps for a good person one would dare even to die—but God shows his love for us in that while we were still sinners, Christ died for us. Since, therefore, we have now been justified by his blood, much more shall we be saved by him from the wrath of God. For if while we were enemies we were reconciled to God by the death of his Son, much more, now that we are reconciled, shall we be saved by his life. More than that, we also rejoice in God through our Lord Jesus Christ, through whom we have now received reconciliation (Rom. 5:1-10).

Now, after reading this passage, just imagine that you are in the center of a courtroom. The proceedings are all based on you. Your attorney is Jesus, and God the Father is the Judge. Jesus proclaims to God the Father that His blood sacrifice applies to you too; there is a legal mandate that now requires an offer of reconciliation from God to you. This offer would be an extension of grace. God the Father agrees and offers you this reconciliation. If the offer had not been given, then you would have been dead in the water. But because grace was extended, you now have a choice.

Do you accept the offer, and all the implications that come along with it, or do you not accept it? This choice is called faith; it's your response to what God has done, is doing, and will do on your behalf. If you decide to accept this reconciliation, a document is officially signed by you and God and written in the blood of Jesus. It's legally binding, unable to be overturned by any other law, and thus your legal status has officially changed. This is what justification is like. It's a legal proceeding of sorts.

However, this is only the beginning. Remember the whole notion of being born again? That is one of the implications of entering this legally binding agreement with God. The construct of who you are will be changed. Why? Because God cannot have a binding relationship with a sinful being. Therefore, this salvation process continues to work, changing you from the inside out. This part of salvation is called sanctification, the process of being made holy.

Being made new is a process that requires a whole-soul involvement, or as the Bible says, transformation. The Greek word translated as "transformed" is *metamorpho*, from which we get the term metamorphosis. It is much like a caterpillar that builds a cocoon around itself, and after a certain period of time, breaks through the cocoon, a much different butterfly.

In the process of sanctification, what really happens is a Spirit-charged transformation of who you are. This includes a change in your temperament, personality, desires, abilities, attraction, etc. Everything changes when you are transformed by God.

Consider this passage:

Do not be conformed to this world, but be transformed by the renewal of your mind, that by testing you may discern what is the will of God, what is good and acceptable and perfect (Rom. 12:2).

One facet of transformation is the mind. According to this Scripture, the mind prior to transformation has an awful bit of trouble discerning anything that is of God. This is remarkably interesting, as we have a world full of PhDs who have studied the Bible and the Scriptures exhaustively, and yet God is declaring here that without a relationship with Him, those people will lack major elements in knowing God and His will.

Logical head knowledge does not equate to full-scale knowledge of God. Therefore, in this sanctification process, someone who knows very little about the academics of Scripture could very well know far more about God than those with fancy letters after their names. Case in point, the twelve disciples–turned–apostles were much like that when compared to the Sanhedrin, which consisted of the religious elite.

Another component in this whole process is glory. Second Corinthians 3:18 states,

> *And we all, with unveiled face, beholding the glory of the Lord, are being transformed into the same image from one degree of glory to another. For this comes from the Lord who is the Spirit.*

Glory is an essential part to the salvation process of being made new. Here we see once again that we are being transformed, but in this regard, we are changed from one level of glory to a higher level of glory.

This begs another question: What in the world is glory? The Hebrew word for glory used throughout most of the Old Testament is *kavad*, or a form of it. The base meaning of kavad is "to be heavy" or "to be honored." Considering this meaning, it is not out of line to see glory as a distribution of weight or clout. Consider the message God delivered to Moses in regard to Pharaoh:

And I will harden Pharaoh's heart, and he will pursue them, and I will get glory over Pharaoh and all his host, and the Egyptians shall know that I am the Lord. And they did so (Ex. 14:4).

What God is saying here is that Pharaoh thought his strength was enough to destroy God's people, but he didn't yet fully understand with whom he was dealing. God has infinitely more weight than Pharaoh did, and once God acted, Pharaoh would receive a full recognition of that. Or in other words, he would give God glory.

God's weightiness in all creation is simply no match for anything else. He has more glory than anything. But do we recognize it? We often see in Scripture that God says, "I will get the glory," or, "They shall behold My glory." It's no coincidence that after those words are spoken, there is usually some catastrophic event and/or a lot of people die.

This can be a bit terrifying to think about, but don't forget the destiny of the believer in all of this. Believers are to be transformed into a greater glory, to become more and more like the image of Christ. Whatever clout or weight we have in this universe right now will substantially increase as we begin to change into the people God has really designed us to be. This is best described in 2 Corinthians 4:16–18:

So we do not lose heart. Though our outer self is wasting away, our inner self is being renewed day by day. For this light momentary affliction is preparing for us an eternal weight of glory beyond all comparison, as we look not to the things that are seen but to the things that are unseen. For the things that are seen are transient, but the things that are unseen are eternal.

There we have it! This transformation process has an end result: being changed to the point that our weight of glory cannot be compared to anything we see today. This, in its entirety, is the final part of salvation called glorification. For this reason, I believe the early church followers were more than content to go to their deaths in the name of Christ. They truly believed in this good news—and this good news can start for you right here and right now. The gospel means that you can become a radically different person today!

5

The Radical Gospel, Continued

After reading the previous chapter, perhaps you have had the realization that there is more to the gospel than most people thought. The truth is, there is! The gospel is the component of God's plan for this earth that, once applied, changes everything. The next three parts to the gospel show what further changes God has in mind for you.

4. We can have a family relationship with God.

Another layer in this good news is the notion that we will become part of the family of God. This is a legal component, but it is also a very personal component. Why is family so important to God?

Family goes beyond a mere physical construct. I can create an invention, putting major effort into its design, pouring my heart and soul into the work of it. Yet if someone were to make me choose between the well-being of my son and the well-being of my invention, my priority would be clear. My son will always come first, over anything like that, because there is a tightknit love and responsibility associated within a family. I am close to my family in ways in which I am not close to other people or things.

In the same way, God may have made us a new creation. Our legal status of righteous may have been signed with

Jesus' blood. But those things were done only so that we might be once again close to God. He didn't do it for the mere sake of design. He did it for the relationship. If we are to be close to God, there is no better representation of closeness than to be joined into His own family.

This is a status that is highly regarded, as no other thing in all creation has the right or privilege to be considered a family member of God. In the context of value, just think of how valuable this familial relationship is to God. He created each and every one of us from nothing, He instilled in us His own image, and when we turned our back on Him, He spent the subsequent six thousand years calling us back to Him in various different ways. It all culminated in Him sending His own Son to be sacrificed on our behalf, in order that we might return once again into His family. What an incredible display of value He regards us with!

From a human perspective, if you lost your child, what measures would you take to get them back? It is really interesting that when we see other people's kids go missing, we sympathize and perhaps empathize with them, but other people's kids do not instill in us the urgency and priority that our own children do. Yet God urgently seeks out those who are no longer His kids, so that He might once again make them His kids. From a human perspective, that is a remarkable action. The people who have been rejecting Him are the very ones He is going after. Salvation is for everyone, not just the favorable ones.

Therefore, the salvation process is first legal, then transformative, resulting in something familial. Romans 8:13–23 helps to explain this concept:

For if you live according to the flesh you will die, but if by the Spirit you put to death the deeds of the body, you will live. For all who are led by the Spirit of God are sons of God. For you did not receive the spirit of slavery to fall back into fear, but you have received the Spirit of adoption as sons, by whom we cry, "Abba! Father!" The Spirit himself bears witness with our spirit that we are children of God, and if children, then heirs—heirs of God and fellow heirs with Christ, provided we suffer with him in order that we may also be glorified with him. For I consider that the sufferings of this present time are not worth comparing with the glory that is to be revealed to us. For the creation waits with eager longing for the revealing of the sons of God. For the creation was subjected to futility, not willingly, but because of him who subjected it, in hope that the creation itself will be set free from its bondage to corruption and obtain the freedom of the glory of the children of God. For we know that the whole creation has been groaning together in the pains of childbirth until now. And not only the creation, but we ourselves, who have the firstfruits of the Spirit, groan inwardly as we wait eagerly for adoption as sons, the redemption of our bodies.

It is vitally important to first understand that crying, "Abba! Father!" is about as personal of an interaction there is. Too many people view the title of Father when referring to God as a title of respect, or an official title, like Father Time or Father Christmas. Yet what this passage depicts is reminiscent of a young child calling to his or her daddy. It echoes a closeness between father and child that is very personal and unique. This is the kind of relationship that God the Father wants to have with us. He is not merely a neutral authority here. He is a loving Dad who wants the very best for His children.

Speaking of the very best, what does that look like? Well, according to this scripture, we aren't just children in a design sense; rather, we are heirs to the kingdom of God. We have an inheritance. This inheritance includes fully redeemed bodies, an increase in glory, and a creation that is eagerly waiting for us to be presented to it as the children of God. In other words, God's family doesn't live in squalor. He doesn't allow for them to be hindered by pain, sin, and death. The believer's inheritance is partly being upgraded into a state of living that defies our earthly comprehension. God's family looks the part of something divine, all-powerful, all-knowing, and thoroughly good. To be a member of God's family brings joy unspeakable, peace that surpasses all understanding, an eternal weight of glory, and a name better than sons and daughters.

This identity cannot be fully realized on earth in mortal bodies that are surrounded by sin. Isaiah 56:1–5 gives us insight into this when it says:

> *Thus says the Lord: "Keep justice, and do righteousness, for soon my salvation will come, and my righteousness be revealed. Blessed is the man who does this, and the son of man who holds it fast, who keeps the Sabbath, not profaning it, and keeps his hand from doing any evil." Let not the foreigner who has joined himself to the Lord say, "The Lord will surely separate me from his people"; and let not the eunuch say, "Behold, I am a dry tree." For thus says*

the Lord: "To the eunuchs who keep my Sabbaths, who choose the things that please me and hold fast my covenant, I will give in my house and within my walls a monument and a name better than sons and daughters; I will give them an everlasting name that shall not be cut off."

This idea of legacy is so distorted in our own worldview that we think legacy actually exists upon this sin-corrupted earth. People are so concerned about having kids to perpetuate their name, so it won't get lost in history. People are so concerned about their national and community identities so the memory of them will last forever. Yet history has shown that all of this is fleeting. Trying to have a legacy in the context of sin is a foolish thing to attempt.

God has a different viewpoint altogether. He calls us to "keep justice and do righteousness," for blessed is the man who does this. Those who do this build a name for themselves in heaven, not on earth. From an earthly perspective, the foreigner and the eunuch are to be pitied because the eunuch will not have a genealogical legacy and the foreigner's national legacy will always be something different from a pure blood association. But to God, both of those people may very well have an eternal hand (memorial) and a name in the house of God, which is better than sons and daughters. Their legacy is assured forever.

The Jewish nation of Israel has echoed this concept well in naming the Holocaust museum *Yad VeShem*, which means "a hand and a name." They take this directly out of Isaiah, and their point in using it is to say that as long as Israel exists, those who died in the Holocaust will never be forgotten. As

The Radical Gospel, Continued

you walk through the museum, at the very end, there is a cylindrical library full of books, and all that is written in the books are the names of the victims. They have a hand and a name from our worldly perspective, but even that display of love and legacy pales in comparison to what God says to those who keep justice and do righteousness, waiting for the completion of His salvation.

The legacy of the family of God will be like nothing anyone has ever experienced before. It is so tremendous that all of creation waits with longing for the revealing of the children of God. During the millennial reign of Christ, I imagine there will be people on the earth who will look to God's children in wonder and amazement over the sight and recognition that they have. Everyone will know who the children of God are and all that implies.

Of all the aspects of the gospel message, this is truly the part that ought to create the most excitement among those who believe. Not everyone has experienced a good family, but everyone knows what a family is. Yet for all the knowledge we may have about family, God's family will blow those expectations out of the water. Family with God will be everything we have always wanted in a family here on earth and infinitely more. It will be relational perfection.

5. Evil will be dealt with.

This is by far the most ignored and rejected part of the gospel message among modern-day believers. The idea that God would specifically have the desire to end evil in a violent way has become anathema in many Christian groups today. Yet the central irony of this viewpoint is that a large portion of the Bible, as we know it, points to this end of time–culminating event when God's conclusion to this current earth will be saturated in violence. And not just any violence—much of it will be God orchestrated.

The God of mercy and grace whom we have come to know and trust is not devoid of judgment and violence. This God in whom we believe is also wrathful. If we choose not to believe this, then we are effectively communicating that we do not appreciate the Bible as an authority. If we love a loving God, then we must love a wrathful God as well because such a God is one and the same. Remember, He is a righteous Judge as much as He is a loving Creator.

So yes, part of the gospel message is that God will eradicate sin and evil from the earth. It will happen, but fair questions to ask are: why hasn't it happened yet, and why doesn't He eradicate sin and evil at a more acute and localized level?

Second Peter 3:9–11 gives us good insight into this:

The Lord is not slow to fulfill his promise as some count slowness, but is patient toward you, not wishing that any should perish, but that all should reach repentance. But the day of the Lord will come like a thief, and then the heavens will pass away with a roar, and the heavenly bodies will be burned up and dissolved, and the earth and the works that are done on it will be exposed. Since all these things are thus to be dissolved, what sort of people ought you to be in lives of holiness and godliness....

God has an amazing level of patience. Another term for it is long-suffering. Why does He allow evil to exist throughout the world? Because people have free will to choose evil, and free will must exist in order for people to make a true choice

The Radical Gospel, Continued

to follow God or not. This choice is so valuable to God that it is worth all the evil and suffering, just so that a few more might find repentance. Make no mistake about it, though, His wrath is growing, and it will someday reach the point of bringing judgment upon the earth. Much like a thief comes when no one expects him, God's wrath will come quite abruptly. Zephaniah 1:14–18 gives us a very sobering image of what that will look like:

> *The great day of the Lord is near, near and hastening fast; the sound of the day of the Lord is bitter; the mighty man cries aloud there. A day of wrath is that day, a day of distress and anguish, a day of ruin and devastation, a day of darkness and gloom, a day of clouds and thick darkness, a day of trumpet blast and battle cry against the fortified cities and against the lofty battlements. I will bring distress on mankind, so that they shall walk like the blind, because they have sinned against the Lord; their blood shall be poured out like dust, and their flesh like dung. Neither their silver nor their gold shall be able to deliver them on the day of the wrath of the Lord. In the fire of his jealousy, all the earth shall be consumed; for a full and sudden end he will make of all the inhabitants of the earth.*

The Great Day of the Lord is a recurring theme throughout the Old Testament, and the New Testament references a final culminating event in which God's justice and wrath are finally delivered at full force. During this event, all evil will be purged from the earth and sentenced to eternal consequences. The righteous will be fully redeemed, and salvation will be fully completed. This is just as much a part of the gospel as the death, burial, and resurrection of Jesus. In fact, Jesus has something to say on the topic as well:

> *For as the lightning comes from the east and shines as far as the west, so will be the coming of the Son of Man. Wherever the corpse is, there the vultures will gather. Immediately after the tribulation of those days the sun will be darkened, and the moon will not give its light, and the stars will fall from heaven, and the powers of the heavens will be shaken. Then will appear in heaven the sign of the Son of Man, and then all the tribes of the earth will mourn, and they will see the Son of Man coming on the clouds of heaven with power and great glory* (Matt. 24:27–30).

The whole Bible—including Jesus, the apostles, and the prophets—speaks about this final defeat of evil. It is necessary to God's plan. Because He has told us of it in advance, it ought to be good news for us. However, I will never quite understand how people can look at God's judgment and view it as inhumane. It's as if people think humanity deserves better treatment. Therefore, a prevalent view and practice has been to downplay the judgment of God and highlight the grace and mercy of God. "The love of God outweighs the judgment of God," says the so-called wise and modern man. Yet no one seems to consider God's judgment to exist within the realm of love. He judges because of His love, not apart from it.

The second coming of Christ is just as important as His first coming, and the judgment of Christ is just as much a part of the gospel message as is the mercy and grace of Christ. Those who will not accept that fact do not believe in the true gospel as presented in the Bible. God's dealing with evil once and for all is part of our hope as believers, and that hope is one of the best parts of the good news.

6. We choose when we die.

Death is inevitable, right? Everyone dies. The saying rings true that there are only two sure things in this life: death and taxes. As Solomon said in Ecclesiastes, everyone dies just the same, whether rich or poor, powerful or weak, and so everyone might as well just eat, drink, and be merry. It has become the common understanding that everyone dies, and that we must simply view death as a part of life. But is that really what God wants for us? What if I said that part of the gospel message was that you would be granted the ability to choose when and how you die?

Now, don't mistake what I am saying. I'm not referring to suicide. Suicide is the selfish choice to end your own physical existence. What I am talking about is the choice to separate your spirit from the physical body in order for God to make a new creation within you. So yes, the body is dead to you, although it keeps on functioning.

We find this concept discussed in Romans 6:3–7:

> *Do you not know that all of us who have been baptized into Christ Jesus were baptized into his death? We were buried therefore with him by baptism into death, in order that, just as Christ was raised from the dead by the glory of the Father, we too might walk in newness of life. For if we have been united with him in a death like his, we shall*

certainly be united with him in a resurrection like his. We know that our old self was crucified with him in order that the body of sin might be brought to nothing, so that we would no longer be enslaved to sin. For one who has died has been set free from sin.

Here we see that dying to self is a prerequisite to identifying with Christ. We must do this in order to fully be set free from sin and experience what real life is like. Notice that baptism is a part of this. The actual and symbolic gesture of being laid down into the water and then being pulled back out of the water represents putting to death the old self and then being brought up out of death and into a new life with Jesus. Is baptism a fully symbolic thing? No, I believe that there are spiritual implications to the physical act of baptism. It is a step of faith.

Baptism is a concrete act of obedience that opens the door into a new type of living. Is this to say that one must be physically baptized in water to go to heaven? Absolutely not. But I do believe that God's plan for everyone's life involves this obedient step of faith. Therefore, there are some sort of spiritual and physical consequences for doing it or not. Baptism is our declaration of death. We choose to do it, and God has given us the ability to choose to do it. The promise of dying to ourselves through baptism is that God has promised a launch into a brand new life.

Paul said that Jesus "condemned sin in the flesh." In other words, sin exists and has a home in each person's mortal body. Therefore, when we die to our old selves (our mortal bodies), what we are effectively doing is eternally separating our spirit from our physical structure. God then creates a new identity

The Radical Gospel, Continued

and a new being within the spiritual believer in Jesus. Therefore, Scripture tells us, "So we do not lose heart. Though our outer self is wasting away, our inner self is being renewed day by day" (2 Cor. 4:16). There is a differentiation here between the "outer self" and the "inner self," as if they were two distinct lives. We see this theme of separation developed within Paul's writings.

In Romans 7:14–18, Paul wrote,

> *For we know that the law is spiritual, but I am of the flesh, sold under sin. For I do not understand my own actions. For I do not do what I want, but I do the very thing I hate. Now if I do what I do not want, I agree with the law, that it is good. So now it is no longer I who do it, but sin that dwells within me. For I know that nothing good dwells in me, that is, in my flesh....*

According to Paul, the believer now has an interesting construct. Their identity is no longer within the physical but rather within the spiritual. Therefore, sin that happens beyond the point of conversion is not centered around the person. Sin exists apart from the person. It exists in the old self, in the flesh. Thus, the reason people's physical bodies still die is because that is where sin dwells, and sin cannot enter the kingdom of God.

Again, we have some good news, though. Paul tells us that we are "once to die and then judgment." So, if we have already died to the old self, we shall not die again, even if our physical body wastes away and stops working. Now, to the one who equates death with the physical body ceasing to work, this all sounds rather insane. But at its core, death truly means to be separated from something. In this frame of mind, eternal death would then mean eternal separation from God. Physical death would be separation of the spirit from the body.

Considering this, let's look again at this idea of dying to the old self. In essence, to die to the old self is to preemptively separate the spirit from the body and allow God to make something new of the spirit. That is where our personhood and identity dwells. The body then becomes a rather meaningless thing that still exists but has little to no value within the kingdom of God. Eventually that body will stop working and will decompose, but none of that will be considered death to the believer because he or she will have already died.

Jesus makes a bold claim: "Truly, truly, I say to you, if anyone keeps my word, he will never see death" (John 8:51). Death is not just one simple act, but rather a state of being. Those who died to the old self in following the Word of God shall never see death. Their bodies will stop working, but their spirits will keep on existing and thriving. Death will only get what it deserves: a smelly, decomposed body corrupted by sin. Paul gleefully states:

> *When the perishable puts on the imperishable, and the mortal puts on immortality, then shall come to pass the saying that is written: "Death is swallowed up in victory. O death, where is your victory? O death, where is your sting?"* (1 Cor. 15:54–55).

Believe it or not, God's gospel message to us is that we have the full option to die to death. We can now be forever separated from what has kept us separated from God. Who wants to be divorced from death today and get married to Jesus instead? Death can keep the aches and pains, the disease, the fear, and the turmoil. Instead we get to keep joy and peace, a God who loves us, and a perfect life. Sounds like an excellent divorce settlement to me!

The Radical Gospel Is...

God fixes everything! That is the gospel. We distorted and corrupted all the good and amazing things that God created. This amazing God could have started over with a clean slate, but instead He placed Himself in the midst of this messy world so that He could show His glory to all. He gave abundantly to us so that we could once again experience the close relationship with Him that He had originally destined us to have. However, part of the process of fixing everything also means that judgment will be cast upon those people who utterly reject Him.

God will fundamentally change the earth back into a state of restored righteousness. Imagine that! Real justice, clean and pure minds and hearts, a government that actually works, and membership in God's family. No sin. No death. No more pain. Everything that we destroyed, God is going to clean right up. Jesus will return and finish what He started two thousand years ago.

Furthermore, God's gospel plan for you means radical change right now. He wants to put a brand-new creation within you that will displace your old self and start to change you from the inside out. The very essence of who you are could be changed into the likeness of Christ. You can be a different and better person. The offer that's on the table here is complete life change, with the promise of a future of glory in the family of God, ruling and reigning with Him over everything. The plan is already in action, and it is moving toward its completion. Do you want to miss out on this type of existence or not? You only have to do three things in order to experience this type of radical change:

1. **Fully repent of your sins:** You must confess before God that you have sinned, that you harbor sin, and that you have been fully corrupted by sin. In humility, you must ask forgiveness for your sins.

2. **Accept the grace of God through the sacrifice of Jesus Christ:** Jesus paid the legal price for you to escape sin. It cost Him His earthly body. Because of that sacrifice, you now have the option to accept that legal freedom. This grace brings you to a state of reconciliation with God.

3. **Give your full allegiance to God as your Lord/Leader:** Once you accept the grace of God, you must also accept that you are a part of His kingdom. You must follow His lead and His commands. He gets your full priority.

If you make this commitment with 100 percent of your being, this is what you can expect to happen:

1. You will die to self, and Jesus will make you alive in a way you never thought possible.

2. The transforming presence of the Holy Spirit will begin to change you from the inside out.

3. You will have a peace and joy that surpasses all understanding.

4. You will have the hope that God will fulfill all of His promises, including:
- Dealing with evil once and for all
- Returning for His people
- Preparing a place for us
- Giving us new, imperishable bodies
- Taking away all pain, sickness, and death

5. You will feel a closeness to God that defies comprehension.

6

A Testimony of Transformation

If you had asked me when I was eighteen years old whether this gospel would truly change my life, I would have laughed and mocked the whole idea. Having grown up in the church, I had prayed the salvation prayer as a third grader and jumped through all the spiritual hoops that I was told to jump through during my childhood and adolescent years. Yet, I never felt like anything really happened. I was expecting some sort of magical, immediate change to occur, and when it didn't, I turned to the older and wiser people in the church. The response that I received from them was disheartening.

No one could articulate their faith to me. No one could tell me what being saved looked like or felt like, except for all the cliché sayings, like, "I now have a sense of peace," or "I just feel better." Salvation was a word that had little meaning in my life; the extent of it was that saved people would go to heaven when they died. It was a frustrating time as I came to the recognition that adults had as little understanding of faith and spirituality as I did. But instead of being honest and straightforward, they tried to play the part of a believer, when they really didn't know what they believed or why they believed it. They were truly the hypocrites that the world blames Christians of being.

So there I was, a high school kid growing up with all the

A Testimony of Transformation

right "church" answers to everything but lacking the essence of what it really meant to believe. It certainly wasn't for a lack of trying, as I must have read through the Bible at least twenty times throughout high school in order to be sufficiently knowledgeable. It didn't work. I attended all church functions I could, trying to find someone who could teach me. It didn't work. I prayed diligently with the hope that I would hear from God and He would answer me. What I got was crickets.

After a childhood of practicing, experimenting, and largely faking my spirituality, I finally gave up at the age of seventeen. All church was to me at that point was a good social institution that helped to produce well-functioning members of society. I was okay with that idea, so I remained in church, but belief in God was not on the table. My belief was in myself, to create my own future and my own way in life.

After working a decent but ultimately dead-end job for two years and surviving three really bad relationships in that same time period, I realized that I was not very good at running my own life. I had no life goals, no passion moving forward, and zero ability to find a good woman and work toward marriage. All I had was a dead-end job, a couple of community college courses under my belt, and the stark realization that I was lost, depressed, and just about ready to give up on life. I would often ask the question, "What am I living for?" There was no point to my life when it was strictly me running it.

I was about nineteen years old at that point, and I came to a conclusion. If I couldn't run my own life, and if I couldn't keep things in control, then perhaps God could. It was quite the humiliating moment for me, as I had discounted God not long before, but there I was with nowhere else to turn. So, I made a very bold decision. I got on my knees before God and repented of my sins. I proclaimed my belief in Jesus and asked Him to give me the grace of salvation through His sacrifice. Then finally I made a vow to God. I told Him that wherever He wanted me to go, I would go, and whatever He wanted me to do, I would do. For all intents and purposes, I gave Him the rest of my life on this earth. He was in charge of it, 100 percent. At that moment, all the years of reading the Bible, and all the time I'd spent in church wondering about my salvation, came back to me, and there was an immediate change that took place. God finally responded to me!

The Power of an All-In Commitment

One thing I've learned in my walk with God is that He is not at all content with having just part of a person. He wants the whole thing! You will never see it said in Scripture to love the Lord your God with 90 percent of your heart. No! He wants all your heart, soul, mind, and strength. God is patiently waiting for you to give Him all of your being, and He is willing to let you go your own way if that is what you want.

The Christian's problem in all of this can be described this way:

Imagine you are on the edge of a cliff with your back to the edge. God's hands are behind you, big enough to catch you. He tells you to lean back and fall into His hands, and He will take you on the adventure of your life. Excited, you lean back further and further. You put your own hands back and can feel His hands there. You are just about at the point of no return, when suddenly the toes of your feet, the last thing touching the cliff, dig in for dear life. So, here you find yourself mostly in the hands of God, but still attached to the cliff He told you to leave. Do you think God is going to take you anywhere while you are still attached to the cliff?

This is where I believe most Christians find themselves. They have sort of committed to God or the idea of faith, but they haven't fully committed. People wish to hold on to too many things in this life instead of giving everything to God. You may be clinging to money and possessions, but you could also be holding tight to relationships, addictions or habits, political ideologies, etc. If you hold any part of your life back from God, why should you be surprised when it seems He doesn't hear your prayers or communicate with you? Why are you surprised when you don't feel the peace and joy that others do?

Christians today need to get past the notion that they can commit only part of their lives to God and keep everything else for themselves. Much like His words to the rich young ruler, Jesus is telling us to give up everything and come follow Him.

I learned this lesson the day I committed my life to God, and I can say with absolute sincerity that it has made all the difference.

Immediate Changes…

Once I made my vow to God and fully committed my life to Him, I received an immediate response from Him. He told me, "You are going to speak about Me in front of people." Now I know this might seem somewhat generic, but this is actually a true miracle because I had zero ability to speak in front of people up to that point. In fact, I had failed about every oral presentation I had to give in school. I would get up in front of people and just freeze. So, when God informed me that I would be speaking about Him in front of people, I made the foolish decision to say, "God, I don't think You understand my situation."

The words hadn't left my mouth when suddenly a passion and a desire rose up within me to speak in front of people. I suddenly had the courage to step in front of people, a bravery that had not existed in me before. I can't explain what happened beyond saying that what wasn't there before was suddenly and miraculously there a moment later. From that point on, I didn't question God anymore.

Only a week later, I found myself coming across an Internet ad for a missions program. Like most other ads, I thought nothing of it at first and moved on. However, over the next five or six days, every time I went online, this ad would pop up on my screen.

Remember, this was still the days of dial-up, before Facebook and Google started profiling every aspect of our lives. I kept seeing this ad until I finally turned to God and said, "Is this what I need to do?" I received confirmation from Him and clicked on the ad. It turns out the organization was one of a handful at the time that allowed people without a college degree to participate in a long-term missions program. After that day, I never saw the ad again.

I called the number, and from that point on, it was almost like the whole thing planned itself for me. I picked a location in Europe (because my only stipulation was to not go somewhere overly hot). I was fully funded in a matter of months and hardly had to ask for money. I marked my departure date on the calendar for a year from that point. For the first time

A Testimony of Transformation

in my life, I felt like I had a distinct plan moving forward and goals to reach for. God was doing everything I had only hoped He would do years before.

Another week later, I was at my job working with a new co-worker, and out of nowhere he mentioned I should try out this small Bible college in the area. At this point, I wasn't about to chalk it up as a coincidence, and I told him I would. As I walked into the doors of said college, I distinctly remember thinking and feeling like I had to attend there. It wasn't a preference thing; it was a must-do. Looking back years later, I still highly value that time as one of the key periods of training and preparation I've had in my life. Chalk another one up for God!

Finally, as I was attending Bible college and preparing for my mission work that would happen in about a year's time, one more thing happened while I was at a church college group meeting. This girl walked in...

Now, before I go into all the fantastic details about the girl, I feel it is vitally important to highlight that within three months of my conversion and commitment to God, I went from being a lost and depressed young man to having a goal and a mission, the miraculous ability to speak in front of people, and doors being opened right and left by God Himself.

This is reality! There is a God who does, indeed, act in such a way as to radically change your life. But it all comes down to the question, What level of commitment are you willing to make? I chose 100 percent, putting all of my cards on the table—holding nothing back—and the result was everything I could have hoped it to be; in fact, it was miraculous! So, what commitment are you willing to make?

Learning to Love

So, there was this girl who walked into a rather small college group at church, and something strange happened. It was like time shifted into slow motion, and a heavenly light shown down upon her. I know this sounds cliché, but it really kind of felt like that—as if it were her and me in a room with no one else. Of course, she didn't see me at all and kept on walking! Immediately I thought to myself, *What's this all about?* It's not like there weren't other very beautiful young women in the church, but none of them prompted that sort of reaction in me. Regardless, there was one thing I knew: I had to ask her out.

I nonchalantly traipsed my way over to a group adjacent to the one that she was in. I have no clue if anyone even tried to talk to me because I was only concerned with one thing: hearing her voice and learning something about her. As I waited for her to speak, it felt like an eternity. The excitement was building as I waited to hear those first words. I leaned in a bit, and the very first words I heard this beautiful lady say, in a soft, sweet voice, were… "My fiancé is overseas in Iraq."

What!? Holy backfire, Batman! That is not what was supposed to come out of her mouth! I quickly exited the area so as to not make a scene, and later that day, I went to God in prayer. *What was that, God? The woman of my dreams walks into the same room as me, and You let this happen?*

Without missing a beat, God spoke to me again and said, "So, what do you care? I thought you had committed to following Me, not her?"

Oooohhhh, well played, God.

He continued, "Did you ever think about talking with Me about this whole situation before you approached her?"

A Testimony of Transformation

It was then that I realized the level of devotion I needed to have toward God. It was easy to follow Him when my life was in turmoil, but now that good things were happening, it was on me to follow Him with just the same level of passion. I apologized for not turning to Him first. I then asked if there was a woman out there for me. He responded by saying, "Maybe, maybe not—but if you trust Me, your life will be enjoyable either way." I was content with that answer, and life went on.

About three more weeks went by, with no sign of this lady at church. I considered that a blessing because if she had been there, it would have made the church group a bit awkward for me. Yet the Sunday after those three weeks, in walks THE girl. I didn't know what to do except to go over and talk with the other people in the room.

As I did so, I noticed that she had walked over and was talking with someone who was standing right next to me. I felt a bit of déjà vu, as this was very similar to the first encounter. I heard someone ask her how her wedding plans were going. Then, to my surprise, she said, "I'm no longer engaged. He broke it off."

I'd be lying if I said there wasn't a party going on inside my mind. I couldn't believe it! When do second chances like this really happen? I was ecstatic, but I also remembered what God had told me. This time I went to Him first and asked if this was right. Should I pursue a relationship with her?

He said to go ahead, but there was a condition: If we started dating, she would have to know from the beginning that God was my number-one priority and not her. So, I spent the next couple of months getting to know her. I found out her name was Stephanie, and I learned a lot about her family. We would hang out wherever and whenever, and she quickly became one of my best friends. But looming over my head was still the issue of dating and marriage. I had had various bad dating experiences in the past, and I didn't want to see that replicated with Steph. So, I devised a brilliant, foolproof plan...which is code to mean that it was actually a terrible plan, but the nineteen-year-old me thought it was brilliant.

I used to play church league basketball in those days, and I determined that the best way to really know if Steph was ready to take the next step with me would be for her to see me at my most unflattering—and still say yes. This was my way of measuring her level of commitment. Yes, I know—terrible plan! But regardless, I played a full game of basketball. I was sweaty and smelly and tired. Pleasant was not a word that could describe any part of me at that moment. And that is when I did it! I walked Steph out to her car right after the game, and I asked her if she would like to go out on a date with me.

The response I received was a confidence-inducing, "Yeah, I guess so." Hey, I'll take it! And forevermore, the Derowitsch method of asking a girl out will have a 100 percent success rate...because I just don't see anyone else trying it. Yet it worked for me.

I was finally going out on a date with Steph, and things couldn't have been better. That is, until I remembered what God had told me. I was going to have to tell her, the person I had really come to love as a friend, even more than a friend, that she would never be the most important person in my life.

We had gone out to eat and were driving back in the car

when I stopped her in her tracks. I asked her what she expected out of our relationship. She seemed blindsided by the question, and said, "I'm not sure—what about you?"

Here it was, the moment of truth. What came out of my mouth next would either destroy whatever we might have had, or God would come through and this whole thing would work out brilliantly.

I looked at her and said, "There are three things you need to know. First, I'm in this for marriage, and if that's not for you, we might as well end this now. Second, God is the most important Person in my life, and you will always be in second place to Him. Finally, I made a vow to God and told Him I would go wherever He wanted me to go and do whatever He wanted me to. He has called me to the mission field, and I'm leaving in six months. If you are okay with everything I just said, and you are willing to do this with me, I'm all in."

There it was, I had said it. It was out there now, and all I had left to do was wait for the hammer to drop. I remember a long pause—and why wouldn't there be one? I had basically told this girl that she has to take a second-place seat to God. How do you respond to that? I sat there mulling over the myriad ways she could go about dumping me and expecting the worst.

Finally, she spoke, and I felt like my stomach was in my throat I was so nervous. Her words pierced the silence: "I think I'm okay with that."

I was so expecting her to turn me down that I almost said, "Well, I'm sorry to hear that." I had to stop myself and realize the magnitude of what had just happened.

"You mean, you're in this with me—through everything?"

She replied with an immediate, "Yeah."

I tried to keep calm, but I was about the most excited I had ever been. I had never thought a couple months before that this was where I would be. This was the defining moment when I truly began to understand love, and since that time, I have been learning something new about it every day.

What Is Love?

I don't care what PhDs, theologians, therapists, or counselors have to say about what love is. The truth is that love is virtually undefinable. Whoever says otherwise is full of hogwash. In fact, from a biblical perspective, there is only one verse of Scripture that can really give us a true definition of love. First John 4:7–8 states,

> *Beloved, let us love one another, for love is from God, and whoever loves has been born of God and knows God. Anyone who does not love does not know God, because God is love.*

John gives us a clear understanding here that love only exists as it comes from God. For God is love—there is the definition. The very nature of God is love. Do you see why I say this is a virtually undefinable word? It's because if we want to be able to fully define and understand love, we must fully define and understand the nature of God—and God's nature is infinite. Defining love in our current state is an impossible task. We continue to use this one word to describe our desire for our children, for our spouses, and for tacos. It doesn't seem quite right to compare the three in this way, but in all reality, it is right. For here is what the Bible says love can look like: patience and kindness (1 Cor. 13:4); self-sacrifice (2 Cor. 5:14); affection (1 Pet. 5:14); taking on another's burdens (1 Cor. 13:7); belief (1 Cor. 13:7); desire (Phil. 4:1); humility (John 12:25); being considerate (Rom. 12:10); seeking good (Rom. 12:9); intimacy and sexuality (Song of Songs 4:10); unity (Eph. 4:16); friendship (Gal. 5:14); discipline (Heb. 12:6); punishment (Heb. 12:6); judgment (Is. 16:5); righteousness (1 John 2:15); compassion (1 John 3:17); salvation (1 John 4:10); gentleness (1 Cor. 4:21); and obedience to God's Word (1 John 2:5).

Believe it or not, this is a rather short list. Love is described in various ways in Scripture, but to define love leaves us with one glaring reality: Love is a mystery! How love affects human beings is a mystery. What love does to transform people is a mystery. Only one thing is sure: This mystery will not be solved by an academic analysis or a scientific experiment. It will only be discovered through an ongoing relational experience.

I said I have been learning something new about love each day since the time Steph and I had that talk because love is far beyond what we can comprehend in any given moment. It's the never-ending discovery of who God is.

This is not to say we cannot experience true and real love even though we cannot know it exhaustively. The fact that love presents itself in so many ways in Scripture gives us the opportunity to participate in love in vastly different contexts.

For example, when talking about God as a loving Creator, love is depicted as self-sacrifice, the desire for closeness, a deep caring for others, and a desire for healing. This is one of the primary ways God describes love in His revelation to us, but that does not mean it is the full extent of love.

Thus, the couple on their honeymoon will participate in

love, as will the martyr who was beheaded by ISIS for his faith. Those people who enjoy and desire a good taco also participate in love, as do those who give up their time and energy and effort for a friend. Among the various ways to experience love, one thing is certain: Love can be distorted in just as many ways. What I've learned over many years is that most people who use the word love truly have a distorted view of love, and what they experience of "their love" is usually destructive.

My commitment to God was so vitally important to my faith walk. I never really experienced true love until I was walking fully with God and fully apart from the world. As my story continues, this learned love would be put to the test.

God Is My Priority

After that night in the car, my relationship with Steph really began to get serious. It wasn't long before we were thinking about marriage and the future. However, one looming issue kept hovering over our heads: the mission field.

I had talked with the agency and learned that my original destination would not work. They told me to say good-bye to Europe and say hello to China. I wasn't too eager to go to Asia, but as it was God's will and not mine, I accepted.

As the months rolled along, everything was moving forward like a well-oiled machine. College was good. My job was good. My relationship with Steph was great. It had only been about six months since I had committed my life to God. In that period of time, I had gone from lost, depressed, and having no discernible future to happy, joyful, and having my future laid out right in front of me.

What a miraculous turn of events! The next months

leading up to August were some of the most memorable of my life. Everything was new and exciting. Life had a zest to it that I had not experienced before. But then the day came. August arrived before I knew it, and I had to do the most counterintuitive things I could imagine. I had to quit my job, take a break from school, and show Steph that I really loved her by hopping on a plane and quite literally flying to the farthest most point on the planet away from her.

She knew that God was my priority, but we had never actually had it put to the test. Now we did, and looking back with hindsight, that was one of the best decisions I have ever made. My love for Steph was and is contingent on my relationship with God. If I had turned my back on God at that time, I would have set our relationship up for disaster. I simply could not do that. So, we said good-bye and promised to wait out the time I was away. This was a giant leap of faith.

7

A Testimony of Happiness and Ministry

China

After a short, little thirty-eight-hour trip filled with planes and airports, I finally touched down in Xiamen, China. I remember stepping off the plane and into a wall of torture. It was 120 degrees with 100 percent humidity. Knowing my one stipulation had been that I didn't want to be placed in a hot environment, I looked up to heaven and squinted so I could just make out God laughing at me. As it turns out, it is not such a good idea to tell God what you are and are not going to do.

I sighed with annoyance and worked my way toward the exit of the airport, met the missionary under whom I was assigned, and started the trip to the town where I would be working. I watched as we drove down various roads. All around me were large cement buildings. There was so much smog in the air, it just about blotted out the sun. All the creeks and rivers looked green from sewage. There was dust everywhere, and people seemed to be living in homes with dirt floors. It was a stark contrast to the climate and lifestyle in Oregon that I was used to, and it made me think, *Toto, we're not in Kansas anymore.*

A Testimony of Happiness and Ministry

My resolve didn't waver, however, as I was there to serve God, not myself. I was driven to the apartment building where I would be living on the top floor for the next seven months. The first test I had in China took place on my second night there. While I was sleeping in my new apartment, a couple of local guys jumped onto my roof from an adjacent building, broke into my apartment through the balcony door, and robbed me at knifepoint. Thankfully, they only took my money, and there was no physical altercation. Yet, if I ever wanted a wake-up call as to the serious nature of where I was and what I was doing, that was it!

I spent seven months there, teaching English at a private school and also at some local colleges. Of course, China is a closed country to the gospel, and missionaries are not allowed to be there as such. Therefore, my primary job was to be an English teacher. What I did on my off time was to provide assistance to Bible studies and cell churches.

In China, there were two types of churches: cell churches and government-sanctioned churches. The government-sanctioned churches were rather large and well attended, but they had some key problems. To start, the government controlled everything they did. So, the average government-sanctioned church could not preach the books of Genesis or Revelation, or any of the miracles of Jesus. Why? Because the government is the beginning and the end in China, and anything miraculous that happens can only be attributed to them. This was the mind-set of the government-sanctioned church.

On the other hand, cell churches were small, and they met randomly since they were illegal. However, they preached the whole truth. This caused a moral dilemma among most of the Chinese that I met while I was there. None of them wanted to break the law, but at the same time, they really wanted to know the real truth. As I witnessed this dynamic unfold over months, I began to understand what the persecuted church experienced. But nothing would prepare me for what was about to take place in my own life.

The Night I Will Never Forget

One night, after a day of teaching, I heard there was going to be a speech at the main university in the area. The talk of the town was that an unsanctioned Christian speaker would be talking about the Bible. This type of event was almost unheard of there, and so many of us Chinese English teachers were eager to attend.

We went to the campus that night. The event was to be held in a small commons area, a building that might fit two hundred people. We walked in to a crowd of people packed like sardines. The room was filled beyond capacity. We worked our way to a corner of the room where there was one line of chairs set up. Being the only white guy there, I was offered the seat of honor closest to the stage. My fellow English teachers and I sat down.

The event began with worship, and right off the bat I knew the entire evening was going to be rough. The sound system kept acting up; it would turn off and back on repeatedly. It was virtually impossible to hear what anyone was saying through the mics. Everything seemed unorganized, and I was quickly beginning to become judgmental of the whole thing.

Finally, the speaker got up, and she struggled through everything she said. It was as if this was her first time speaking in front of anyone. Adding the sound system problems on top of that, it was actually painful to hear her speak. One of the Chinese teachers was translating for me, and I remember that her message was regarding the gospel, but to this day I couldn't tell you what she said. When the presentation finally ended, I was relieved and annoyed at the same time: relieved that it was over, and annoyed that my whole evening had been wasted on it.

We all got up and moved toward the exit. As I walked through the door to the street, I was absolutely awestruck. There must have been ten thousand people filling up the street and surrounding the little commons building. We asked some of the people what they were there for, and they said that they had come to hear the truth.

Ten thousand people were crowding around this little building, hoping and yearning to hear just a snippet of the truth. And there was I, a selfish young man who was judging and ridiculing the whole thing, simply because I was inconvenienced.

That night was the only time I ever cried while in China. I had suddenly realized the power of Jesus' words: "Blessed are the beggarly in spirit, for theirs is the kingdom of heaven" (Matt. 5:3). If the true desire of a person's heart was to know God, to know the truth and seek after it wherever and however they could, then they would take joy in the truth, regardless of the production of an event. Those people wanted truth like a beggar wants bread, and I was like the rich man who scoffed at the beggars. That was one of the most humbling experiences of my life.

I was committed to following God, but I didn't have the passion for His life-changing grace that these Chinese people did. It tore me up on the inside, but that night I changed.

Nevermore would I be too good or too smart for the truth. The counterintuitive nature of God says that if you want to taste heaven on this earth, you must first be a spiritual beggar. There is no way around it, and no way to avoid it. The truly happy people on this earth have taken up the habit of approaching God with a humble and beggarly spirit.

I realized that night that God had been training me—not necessarily for mission work in China, but for gospel work wherever I was. How could I really communicate the gospel if I didn't fully live the gospel? I left the college campus somewhat depressed, as I fully understood that America was not like China. When my time in China was done, I would go back home to a church culture that was predominantly concerned with entertainment and not the Spirit of Truth. How was I going to declare the message of the gospel in that kind of environment? To this day, wherever I go, that question crops up in my mind and heart.

Learning How To Get Beat Up

The remainder of my time in China was spent training in how to take a beating. Iron Mike Tyson once said, "Everyone has a plan until they get punched in the face." That was my experience—not physically, but spiritually and emotionally.

Since China is a closed country, there were multiple times when the government would shut down the Internet for weeks on end. Of course, my primary method of communication with people back home was through social media. During one span of about six weeks, I had no contact with anyone stateside. It was a time of isolation, depression, and learning how to be content in any situation, as the apostle Paul said.

A Testimony of Happiness and Ministry

Beyond that, the missionary family under whom I was working began to have tumultuous family issues. It eventually caused an unbearable work environment. Because they made up the majority of the white English speakers in the town where we were, I found myself in a situation I really could not back out of. I needed the missionary family, and they needed me too, at least for teaching purposes.

I had to face my problems and speak up when necessary, hold my tongue when prudent, and still serve God. As I look back, I couldn't have asked for better training in how to lead people. As God had taught me, I would never back down from a fight—I would see it through to the end, but the end of a fight did not mean that one was victorious and the other was defeated. Nor did it mean that both people had to be bloodied. The best outcome to a fight was when all parties involved recognized the truth.

In my case, the missionary I worked for became too arrogant in his own estimation to listen to anything. Therefore, I remained silent, did my job the best I could, and waited for God to open a door.

During that time, I endured peer pressure abuse, verbal abuse, zero support (because I was still in a foreign country and didn't adequately speak the language), and, of course, domineering personalities. Many times the missionary raided my apartment because his son was my roommate, and he was concerned about his son using drugs. I was just collateral damage within this family's personal debacles.

However, after I had endured this situation for months, God did open a door when the missionary decided to take his family to Thailand and leave me by myself in China—which wasn't supposed to happen. I prayed to God diligently, and

He finally released me to go home. I finished out that month of work, left the missionary a letter explaining how I felt about the situation, and then hopped on a plane back home.

In February 2007, I returned home worn out, tired, and having lost about forty-five pounds. The only thing that was strong about me was my relationship with God; it had never been better.

Happy Days

After I returned home to the nice, clean atmosphere of Oregon, I discovered that Steph had been faithful to wait for me those seven months. It wasn't easy, but we had both weathered that time away, and I was about to enter what I would consider to be the longest stretch of pure happiness in my life.

I returned to Bible college and established friendships that are still quite close to this day. I got a job working for the post office, which was a perfectly fine change of pace for me. Within six months, Steph and I were engaged to be married. We both were quite involved within our church and college group. Everything was once again working well. I was excited about God's next plan for me, and Steph was excited about becoming a nurse. We were both looking forward to starting our family. Life was good.

Life continued on just like that for the next year. The wedding day came, and I remember it simply being a blur. Steph would even tell you she doesn't remember much from that day. All we know is we got hitched, we had a reception, and then it was over. Steph was, of course, a very beautiful bride, and I managed to be presentable. The family was happy, and we were happy. Then we went on our honeymoon, which was...ahem...everything a couple could hope a honeymoon to be. All that to say, I was really enjoying married life.

But then the honeymoon ended, and we were back to apartment life, making almost no money, and trying to make ends meet working part-time jobs and going to school at the same time. It didn't matter—we were so happy those first months, we didn't even realize how miserable our poverty was. In fact, it wasn't until $8,000 in credit card debt had piled up to supplement our bills that we realized things were at code red status.

The Miracle Job

By this point, it was nearing the end of 2008, and the recession was hitting full-force. My job had cut my hours, and so had Steph's. Yet our rent seemed to magically increase. I guess rentals are recession-proof. We quickly realized that if something didn't change within a month, we wouldn't be able to pay our rent and we would be homeless. As the husband and the provider of the household, I went out looking for jobs, figuring seven years of work experience would land me a job quickly. It only took a few days for me to realize how wrong I was. Nobody was hiring. I had zero options save for one: pray.

Instead of seeking jobs out, I spent the next couple of weeks praying that God would provide for me just as He promised He would. I told Steph (who was understandably freaking out a little bit) that this was a test of our faith, and that we must show God we truly believed what He had told us. So, we prayed and prayed, and even when time was getting rather short, we prayed some more. We put our trust in Jesus, and then something miraculous happened.

I was about four weeks into the fall term of school, and taking a philosophy class from a professor I had known by reputation but had never met in person. Even during the class, I had only talked to him once in passing. One day, this professor made an announcement that there was an opening for a youth pastor at a church about an hour away. It came with a modest monthly salary as well as a parsonage with all utilities and bills paid for.

I looked around the room to see if anyone else heard that because, you know, we were all poor Bible school students, and many were hoping for a paid job in a world where youth pastor experience would be payment enough. Nobody seemed to react. I went up to the professor and told him I was interested in the job, and he put a good word in for me. By the end of that month, I had the job.

This might not seem like a miracle to some people, but knowing that everything we truly needed was provided at just the right time and in a way through which I could gain some much needed experience was very much a miracle. Furthermore, I have never had someone I really didn't know ever recommend me for a job before, and to have no other person interested in the job in a field where those paid jobs are highly sought after was completely illogical to me. It was a move of God and an answer to prayer.

And so I became a youth pastor, and we lived paycheck to paycheck for three years, but there was never any fear of homelessness or a lack of basic needs. We paid off our debt, and we served God as best we could. He came through at the eleventh hour, but everything He said He would provide for was provided. God was faithful!

During those three years, the happiness continued. Steph

and I worked diligently to finish our college educations, we established many new relationships within the church where we were, and we spent time investing in young people's lives. My life at that moment was such a stark contrast to the life I had had prior to committing to God that it felt like a whole generation had passed, even though it had only been about three years. My life was changing day by day.

Children

The capstone to this time of happiness was the birth of our first child, whom we named Cyrus. Steph and I had dreamed of a family for a while, but we were realistic enough to wait until we were in a financially better situation. She had just finished with school the week before we found out she was pregnant.

I cannot speak adequately of the amount of joy and excitement that existed within our home during those nine months of waiting for Cyrus's birth. I fully understand that kids don't always feel like a blessing to some people, especially in certain circumstances. But to us, it was blessings upon blessings.

I cannot forget when Cyrus decided to come into the world, because it was during my finals week in college. I remember distinctly that I had been very sleep-deprived the two nights before, making sure I had studied enough for the tests. I had just finished my last final exam at 10 p.m., when I got the message to get to the hospital. I stood next to Steph for ten more hours of labor, and then our baby boy finally came into the world. The experience was surreal, as I held my firstborn son in my arms. I was full of hope, happiness, fear, and yes, some trembling. For those who have never been in that situation, it is like every possible emotion is somehow shoved into one moment. But above all, I once again experienced a new kind of love.

After having a son, I immediately understood the level of attachment that the Father had to have for Jesus. His willingness to sacrifice His only Son for me brought an entirely new context to my life. The depths to which God is willing to go to pull us out of the trenches hit me like a ton of bricks that morning. I praised God that day for how far He had brought me, and to what He had brought me. Yet that was the last of good things I would experience for quite some time.

Three months later, we found out that Steph was pregnant again. This bit of news was offset by the fact that things at the church had become tense as many families had decided to leave. However, it was business as usual for me as I decided to move forward with my trust in God, come what may. With this attitude, I finished my college degree and immediately geared up for seminary. Summer rolled around quickly, and before we knew it, we were at the twenty-week ultrasound.

8

A Testimony of Enduring through Tragedy

The Worst Day of My Life

I remember sitting with excited anticipation as the technician spread lubricant all over Steph's belly. The technician then put the ultrasound wand onto her stomach and began to move it around to gather an image. Ten seconds went by before we heard the words, "This doesn't look..." He stopped himself, then quickly ran out of the room crying. Steph and I didn't know what to think, as we sat there rather shocked by the whole ordeal.

Ten minutes must have gone by before a doctor walked in and sat down. He told us that our baby had severe swelling all around its body, which was a major sign of Turner's syndrome, a genetic disorder that causes fluid to be improperly regulated in the body. He proceeded to tell us there was a 99 percent chance that our baby would die before birth. He then finished this conversation by suggesting that we get an abortion. Our response was, "Not in a million years, Doc." We then cried a little bit and began to do the only thing we could do: pray and move forward with life.

That afternoon I received a call from the senior pastor, who was unaware of what had just happened. He asked me to come in and meet with him. When we sat down, he proceeded to tell me that the church had lost too many families and could no longer afford to keep me on as a youth pastor. In one horrific day, I was told that my baby would die, my job was over, and we would be forced to move out of our home, the church parsonage.

A week after that was my first orientation day at Western Seminary. I'm sure I looked as though I were absent-minded because I was. My mind and my heart were back with Steph and our daughter in her womb. My stress level was on overload because I didn't know what the next few months were going to bring. In my great stupidity, I tried to push forward with school and not lose a beat due to our circumstances. That lasted a few weeks. I eventually dropped out of that term, and ultimately for the rest of the year. After weeks of prayer and ultrasounds, and watching Steph cry herself to sleep every night, I finally cracked.

When God Does Miracles

A few weeks into this waiting game concerning our baby girl, and I had just about had enough. Each day we prayed. Almost each night, Steph cried herself to sleep. I had a distressed wife, a stressed-out home life, and the looming reality that our time in our home and at that church was very short. A feeling of despair crept in and found its dwelling within me. Everything was going to come crashing down, and there was nothing I could do about it. Prayer was my only option, and it didn't seem to be helping in any sort of way.

One particular night, I had just finished listening Steph cry herself to sleep once again, and I was up until midnight, when I just lost it. Not wanting to wake my family, I left the house and hiked across the field to the church. I let myself in and worked my way to the sanctuary.

Once I entered the sanctuary, I let God have it! Expletives were shooting out of my mouth right and left, and if I repeated anything I said on paper, it would be to my everlasting shame. But I wasn't about to let God off the hook. He needed to know everything I was thinking and feeling. I ranted and raved toward God for about half an hour—some of it in the midst of tears but most of it in anger. God remained silent and still for the entire time I lambasted His name.

When I was finally finished and had spoken my last word, God spoke to me. I couldn't tell you if it was an audible voice or not, but it was so blatantly real it felt like I was speaking to Him face-to-face. He said, "Jayson, your daughter is going to die, and I am not going to prevent that from happening. Do you still love Me?"

Wow! I didn't know what to think. I was so angry with God that a large part of me really didn't want to love Him. However, I really truly believed in who He is and what He said about life and the afterlife. I had really believed and experienced the relationship with Him surrounded by grace. He was my God, and nothing was going to change that! So, I turned to Him after a minute or so of thinking through what He had said, and I responded, "Lord, part of me wants to hate You, but I can't. You are my God, and You have changed my life, and I will love You regardless of what happens to me or my daughter."

Part of me despised what I had just said, but my inner man spoke the truth in that moment. I did love God! Immediately after those words left my mouth, I lost all control of my body and fell to the ground. My body felt weightless, almost like it was being lifted off the ground. All of the burdens and stress, everything I had been carrying on my shoulders, melted away. An amazing warm feeling came over my whole being as I lay there with not a care in the world. What happened next is almost indescribable. The feeling of it was as if God had a great big pitcher full of warm truth, and He began to pour it out on me. As it hit me, it went through my mind and my heart and then utterly surrounded me. It was the truth of who He was, His promises to His people, His commitment to me. There was no room for anxiety or despair within the truth of God.

This experience lasted about three hours. Once it was finished, I was brought immediately back to that cold, drafty sanctuary at about three in the morning. There isn't much more I can say about that evening except I am certain I experienced a supernatural encounter with God, giving me rest and peace. It was as the Scripture says, I had a "peace that surpasses all understanding," because I certainly didn't understand everything that happened. But one thing I knew, when I left the sanctuary that evening, I was okay.

I still had stressful things to deal with, and I still had a tumultuous home environment to reenter. But God had done something in my life that changed me forever, and if there was a way to earn or buy three more hours like that, I would give everything I owned in a heartbeat to have that experience again. I experienced a supernatural miracle from God. It was the gospel working in me during one of my greatest hours of need.

A Testimony of Enduring Through Tragedy

Eden Grace

After that night, I returned to the daily grind of praying, attending weekly ultrasounds, and finishing up my last few days of work. About four weeks later, Eden Grace finally decided to enter this world. Steph had to have an invasive C-section to get her out because she was so deformed. Once they got her out, they walked her quickly over to a small bed where I was waiting.

I watched her take two breaths, and then there was nothing. She was gone. Her body was so swollen that she had no discernible face or arms. The only thing that wasn't swollen was her feet. As I grabbed her little toes, I remember praying to God that I would one day get to see my beautiful daughter without sin distorting and ruining her body. The knowledge that He held her safe and sound gave me the most peace I had experienced since the night God had moved so miraculously.

Steph took many weeks to recover from the surgery, and much of that time was necessary to mend not just her body but also her heart and spirit. As for me, I did something a little different. I found a person who custom-made hiking sticks (I am an avid hiker), and I had him make a stick with this verse carved into it: "Trust in the Lord with all your heart, and lean not on your own understanding. In all your ways acknowledge him, and he will make your paths straight" (Prov. 3:5–6).

I needed something tangible in my life that would constantly remind me of what God had already done for me, and that He was faithful to see me through tough times. At the top of the walking stick, I had the names Jireh, Shammah, Ra'ah, and Tsidkenu carved in it. These are some of the names of God found in Scripture, but they are also promises. They continually reminded me that God would provide, be with me, be my shepherd, and be my righteousness. Even to this day, I still look at the stick from time to time and am astonished at how God has brought me through the muck and the mire.

After those many weeks, a lot of change happened. We officially left the parsonage and moved to the other side of town, into a rat-infested shack of a house. It was all we could afford, and we had come to the conclusion that it would be better if I didn't work while I was in graduate school so I could focus and get my degree done as quickly as possible. So, Steph took on the mantle of provider as she was now a nurse, and I focused on school.

The next few months were rather low-key as I slowly began to get back into school. Cyrus was now a year old, and we were once again moving forward in life with the help of God. A couple more months went by, and we found out some great news. Steph was pregnant again.

Abigail Elise

I knew that if Steph got pregnant again and it was a girl, we were going to name her Abigail, which means "a father's joy." There could be no truer statement made. I was beyond joyous that we were expecting again. Everything looked fine, the early ultrasounds came back normal, and life was good once again. We still walked on eggshells until we made it to that twenty-week ultrasound, which of course was the primary benchmark to make sure the baby would be healthy.

It was the middle of summer, and we had just finished the pivotal ultrasound a week or two before. To celebrate,

A Testimony of Enduring Through Tragedy

Steph and her sisters got together to go to the pool. Meanwhile, my two brothers-in-law and I decided to get out of town and go camping. I hiked with my trusty walking stick, breaking in a new pair of shoes. We were in the wilderness in the mountains near the Oregon coast. We were taking a three-and-a-half mile hike, which was all downhill. I made it about three-quarters of the way when suddenly I stepped and felt excruciating pain in my heel.

When we got back to the campsite, I took my boot off to discover that the outer layer of skin on my heel had completely separated from the rest. In essence, my entire heel had been rubbed raw. I nursed the wound as best I could, but almost immediately it began to swell, and I began to run a fever. We decided to stay the night and head back out in the morning when hopefully things would be better.

That night, without any warning, Steph went into labor about eighteen weeks too soon. She was rushed to the hospital, and the police tried to find us to contact us about what was happening, but we were too far out in the wilderness to have cell reception. Steph's older sister stood by her side as Abigail Elise came into this world. She fought for life for a good half hour, but she had simply come too early. She died that night a fully healthy baby, just not developed enough. I never got to see her alive.

The next morning, we all got up at our campsite, and nothing had changed with my foot. So, I bandaged it up, put my sandals on, and told the other guys I would hike on ahead. I asked them to give me an hour head start because I would be slow. So off I went with my hiking stick, backpack, and faithful dog, Manny, right behind me. Each step was excruciating pain, and after about a quarter mile, the fever and headache came back.

As I hiked farther up the mountain, I came back into the range of cell reception, and I could instantly hear my phone dinging as dozens of texts came in. I reached for my phone and saw the words "It's an emergency," "Get to the hospital," and "Steph is in labor." At that point, I knew that most likely we had lost another child. I could hardly breathe. I couldn't think. I just kept walking because forward was the only way I could go. With my disoriented state of mind, I somehow wandered off the main trail and headed down a side trail. I wasn't paying attention as I kept walking along, but the trail kept narrowing until I reached a point where it was no wider than half my foot, and I reached a very steep edge that went down into a ravine. At that point, I finally realized that I was lost and had to turn around.

I had a sliver of foot space and a dog that didn't know how to lead. Manny tried to walk past me to get behind, but he slipped and fell over the edge. As he went down, he caught my foot and I went down, too. In one swift movement, I plunged my walking stick into the ground as an anchor and laid flat out over the edge. I looked down to see Manny tumble all the way to the bottom. Of course, he was fine, but for me, not so much.

As I lay there clinging to my walking stick, I remember looking up and seeing that verse, and the names of God, etched into the stick. As bad as I felt in that moment, and as much pain as I knew I would experience, I also knew that God's power in me would be enough to overcome it. There I lay, half over a cliff edge, hanging on to a stick, with a swollen foot, a fever, a headache, out in the middle of the Drift Creek Wilderness, and the realization that another child of mine was likely in heaven. I was weak, but I felt strong. I was limping along, but I also felt like I could weather any storm. That was God in me.

I slowly worked my way back to my feet and started to hike back to more stable ground. Manny followed my voice until he found a path that he could run back up. I continued to hike until I heard the voices of my brothers-in-law. They had caught up to me as I found my way back to the main trail. They had also gotten word of what had happened and asked if I wanted to know what had happened. I said no, not until I was out of that place.

When we finally reached the car, it felt as though I had reached the promised land, but a split second later, it felt as though I were entering a hearse. I didn't really talk most of the way back to town. I could only think of Steph in that moment, as I knew she must have been devastated.

Upon arriving at the hospital, I made a beeline right toward the maternity ward and found my way to her room. She had a brave face on, but this time around, there was no rare disease or genetical disorder to reconcile what had happened. It's not like we could say that God was extending grace by not allowing our child to endure a life full of pain and agony. This time around, we didn't have any answers. All we could do was sit together, pray together, mourn together, and hang on to the hope that God would, indeed, bring something good out of this.

I held the body of Abigail in my arms, looking at a beautiful little girl. She had the most peaceful face I think I've ever seen. For the next many nights, I pondered the "if only" questions. If only I could have been there? If only she would have been born three weeks later? If only I could have had the opportunity to get to know her? I certainly felt robbed in the moment, but that feeling wouldn't stay around for terribly long.

As we did with Eden, we went to the cemetery and held a graveside service. I retained the honor of speaking on behalf of my children as I delivered the eulogy, then I gave my little girl a blown-kiss farewell, as I knew and believed that I would see her again someday.

Terrible Illness

Not long after we buried Abigail, I began to have weird health episodes. At first, I had strange panic attacks, where I couldn't breathe well. When I was working or running around, I would be fine. But when I was at rest, these attacks would spring up. I managed them for a while, as they were little more than a nuisance. But after a month or two, suddenly they started happening all the time. It finally got to the point that I would constantly have the feeling like I was only breathing in a quarter of the oxygen I needed.

It became debilitating, and after a few more months, I started to experience extreme fatigue. Some days I couldn't even lift my arms. I would eat about a half a soda cracker a day and be fully immobile, confined to my chair at home. Of course, by this point we knew something was drastically wrong, and we began to look for answers from the doctors. I must have undergone every medical test possible over the course of the next few years as we tried to figure out what was wrong. They all came back normal.

After about a year of this suffering, I began to develop one more terrible symptom: I started to feel nauseous all the time, constantly feeling like I was at the point of throwing up, and often, I did throw up. This was my plight for nearly four years: constant breathing problems, severe fatigue, and nausea and vomiting.

The doctors couldn't figure out what was going on. People started to think I was faking it for attention, or some other weird reason. Even Steph began to get frustrated as I was unable to do much of anything to contribute to the family. I felt like a failure, even though I fully knew what I could and could not do.

I was never suicidal during this time. However, I did suffer from depression, anxiety, and loads of stress. We had mountains of school and medical debt and only one income. We had a young boy to raise. I was still trying to finish my graduate degree, and we would lose four more children during that four-year time span. In this context, there were many nights when I prayed that God would just end my life on this earth and take me home. I certainly felt like I was close to death.

I finally prayed these words, "God, if it's Your will to take me, then please take me. But as it is, my body is still functioning, and I am miserable. If I am to continue on like this, please give me something I can do to make it all worth the pain and toil. Give me a ministry."

Once again, God answered my prayer. He told me to start writing. *But I don't even enjoy writing,* I thought to myself. Yet I took His command and obeyed. I started to write as ideas came. Within a year and a half, I had written my first book. It wasn't anything special or spectacular, but it was confirmation that I could do it. Furthermore, I discovered I actually enjoyed writing. Perhaps it was another God-given gift. Nevertheless, it was then that God gave me an idea to write a fantasy novel about the salvation experience. This task truly helped me get through the remainder of those four years.

Dinah Louise, Israel, and Micah

During those days of illness, we found out we were expecting again. To my great shame, I can't say that I was ever excited during that pregnancy. Between illness, school, and the constant worry that had now become common during Steph's pregnancies, I didn't have much time or energy to be excited.

Steph was put onto bedrest early on, as the doctors were concerned about excessive activity causing early labor. This, of course, put an extra strain within our household, as I couldn't find work in my condition, and now Steph couldn't work either. We were living on a shoestring budget, hoping that our meager savings would hold out for as long as this would take.

The bedrest lasted about four or five weeks, when once again Steph went into early labor. This time, however, I was there for the delivery. Steph had made it to about twenty weeks by the time Dinah Louise decided to enter the world. When she finally came out, she had already passed away. I remember holding her in my hand, as she was small enough to fit in my palm. Who knows what she would have been like? I'm not even sure what she would have looked like as a full-term baby. So many questions rifled through my head, but the one question I wasn't expecting to hear came from our doctor: "I can dispose of that if you like?" she said.

Well, wasn't that just the cherry on the parfait of this whole experience? Our daughter—treated no better than trash during her short time on this earth. Steph and I kindly asked the doctor to leave, but on the inside, we really wanted to scream at her. Yet, my anger was directed at me as much as it was at her because what she said wasn't all that different from what I had felt throughout the twenty previous weeks. Of all our kids, the one I feel the most melancholy toward is Dinah. In my job of being a father, I probably failed her the most of all our other kids.

When it came time for the funeral, I had very few words to say. I remember my parting words were, that much like Jacob's sons and his daughter, Dinah, our Dinah was the one who endured the most neglect, and in that context, her value and worth beamed through it all. The very person who was treated like trash had become the very one who sparked a passion in me to fight for the unborn and the newly born. Dinah's influence still lives on, even though her life is away from this place.

Over the next year and a half, we had two more children. Both were early-term miscarriages. The first we named Israel, and the second we named Micah. Those were some of the very worst days of my life as I thought I was fairly close to death. Almost every day was spent in a chair, lying in bed gasping for air, or with my head over a toilet vomiting. Nothing in my body seemed to work right, and I barely made it through each day.

Graduating and Finding a Cure

In the year 2015, I finally finished my college education. By the pure grace of God and with an immense amount of tenacity, I finished my master's degree with a 3.8 grade point average and high honors. I remember barely making it through the commencement ceremony without falling over or throwing up, but it was done. I had been out of work for four years, and now that I was fully done with school, the pressure was now on to get a job once again.

However, my mysterious illness didn't go away. By this point, I had been suffering from the symptoms for at least two years, with no sign that they would subside. So, I faithfully continued to write, as that was certainly one thing I could do. Two years after I graduated, I had fully published two books. However, they didn't equate to any lucrative money for our household. We still had thousands in medical debt to pay off, and much more in student loans. The weight of that burden continued to haunt me as I did everything I could think of to do to get well again, or to find a paying job I could do while being sick. Nothing seemed to work!

Throughout this time, prayer was my only safety net. It was the one thing I could fall back on and know that on the other end there was a God who still cared about me. Trying to rationalize my illness was a fool's game, as all Scripture pointed to these types of things happening in life. All flesh was corrupt because of sin, and therefore, all flesh would die. It made little difference whether it happened at a young age, in old age, or by what manner it took place. Death would happen because of sin, and I fully knew God would not prevent that from happening. So, I saw my future as completely in the hands of God. Whether I died or lived did not really matter to me. I grew tired of the pain. I grew tired of being debilitated. Yet I never gave up on God.

Finally, after four years of being ill, I started seeing yet another doctor. By this point, I probably had gone to over one hundred doctor's visits trying to glean some insight as to what was going on. They all had brought zero productive solutions. This new doctor was different. He once again suggested that what was happening to my body was originating in my brain, but he explained (in light of my skepticism) what all chemical imbalances in the brain can actually do. I chose to trust his judgment and give his idea a shot.

I started taking different medications that could potentially help chemical imbalances, switching out when certain ones obviously didn't work. It took a year of testing and changing medications before we finally found the one that worked. I started taking it toward the middle of 2017. Within a month, I was back on my feet and feeling pretty good. Within a year, I had no more symptoms. I went from a healthy twenty-six-year-old young man, to spending five years close to death, to then returning to a healthy thirty-one-year-old man.

Lysani

During those latter years of finishing up college and still being very ill, Steph had discovered that she was once again pregnant. This was our seventh child, and the stress of the whole circumstance had never been worse. We were once again excited, but in the back of our minds, we knew the track record. Cyrus was now five years old and getting to be old enough that we simply couldn't continue having more kids with the potential outcome we were used to, for his sake.

So, this child would be our last, regardless of the outcome. We continued to have renewed hope as each passing week went by. Everything seemed to be okay. No abnormalities, no weird circumstances, and our perinatologists even said that nothing appeared to be high risk. Had it not been for our history, there would have been no need for a perinatologist.

All of this continued to reassure us that this time things might be different. Furthermore, I had just finished graduation, which was a huge relief, and Steph had her twenty-week ultrasound again, which came back normal. Life was getting exponentially easier, and it couldn't have come at a better time as my health was still very poor at that point.

Then, when twenty-four weeks came around, Steph once again went into labor. We didn't know what exactly was going on, but there was still some hope, as children have been known survive as early as twenty-four weeks. We waited with gut-wrenching anticipation for what would happen next.

Steph was taken in for an emergency C-section. Our daughter Lysani came into the world shortly after. At first, things looked rather good. But we quickly discovered that something was wrong, and Lysani was fading quickly. Once again, we stood with her, and I held her in my hands as we watched her take her final breaths. Lysani passed away in May 2015 from an E-coli infection.

That was our last child, and to those who may wonder why we continued to have children after the first two passed away, I can confidently say it was a mixture of stubbornness and science. We are actually the 1-in-100-million case where there was no common cause for each child's death. Every doctor we saw was thoroughly dumbfounded that so many abnormal and unique things could happen to one family. But that was us. We lived it, and we weren't about to give up when the next one could be a different story. Yet, when we took our whole family into account, we knew we couldn't put them through any more of the heartache. We buried Lysani next to all our other children, and once again I bid her farewell for a little while.

A Testimony of Enduring Through Tragedy

When Kids Die

"How could you believe in a so-called loving God when He would allow your children to die?" asks the wise modern man. I can't even begin to recount how many times I've heard rhetorical questions like this from people who don't have the faintest clue what they are talking about. Their reactions are priceless when I respond to them by saying, "You have it all wrong. I am exponentially blessed and haven't been more thankful to my God than I am right now."

It's true that losing anybody, especially children, is very painful and sorrowful, and that pain and sorrow doesn't just go away in a couple days. It can sprout up years later at very interesting times and places. Yet my pain and sorrow does not correlate with my belief and love for God. In fact, it's because of my belief in God and His gospel truth that I am being transformed, that I can find immense joy even in the midst of losing so many children.

The truth of God that I hold onto is that my children are redeemed from this world. They are with God, without pain, suffering, or sin. What this means for me is that I am going to have Christmas morning times ten million when I see them again. I am blessed beyond measure because I will never have to know them with a sin nature. I will never have to see them rebel. I will never have to see them suffer from the likes of depression, illness, or abuse.

The first time I will truly get to know my kids, they will be perfect. I will experience their unblemished and godly personalities. I will laugh with them, hug them, play games with them, sing with them, and eat with them, all outside the realm of sin and destruction. The truth of my circumstances is that the more I think about what God is doing in all of this, the more I realize that the poor people are the ones who have to watch their kids grow up and possibly turn to sin and evil, reject God, and become something they were never designed to be.

I've got six kids whom I am guaranteed to see again in heaven! I have one child whom I pray for daily and hope earnestly that I will see in heaven. How many other people can say that about their families? You see, I am exponentially blessed. My kids are with the best Babysitter in the universe, and I don't have to worry one iota about them until I see them next. God has been good to us!

I fully understand that not everyone has the same viewpoint or mind-set that I have on this issue. However, how many of those people are really living out the gospel? How many are being thoroughly transformed from the inside out? How many have been saturated with the truth and fully rely on what God has said? There is a great line of demarcation separating those who *think* gospel and faith and those who *live* gospel and faith.

The Radical Gospel at Work

So, if I claim to live gospel and faith, what is the result of that? What is different in my life compared to other people's lives? How about we start with the fact that I have said farewell to six children over the span of five years, and I am not in a mental/psychological institution? My wife and I have endured immense trauma and illness, and yet we are still happily married. I have had the last half of my twenties seemingly ripped from me, and I still have no regret or resentment.

In fact, my family is doing quite well. We have endured

various trials and come out at the other end better for it. I don't blame God for anything that has happened. Rather, my relationship with Him is the best it has ever been, as He has shown Himself faithful to me. We live. We work. We create things. We rest. We grow in our relationships. We seek to find joy in everything. We worship God consistently. We pray often. This kind of living is a blast!

So, what is the recipe for this kind of success? It starts with a whole-soul commitment to God. This isn't just committing to the idea of God, or even to the notion that He is a ruler over you. This commitment is far beyond what most people are willing to do. It requires that a person surrenders and relinquishes control over every aspect of his or her life.

That means we must surrender our finances, careers, relationships, love lives, emotions, intellects, decisions and wills, physical bodies, and societal status—all are on the altar before God. Absolutely nothing is held back, whether it makes sense or not. A commitment to God means complete surrender to Him and allowance for Him to change us however He wishes. For those who hold back part of their lives from God, they ought not to expect God to do anything transformational. Remember, God doesn't just want a part of you; He wants all of you.

Part of this whole-soul commitment to God requires an absolute reliance upon the truth of His Word. What this means is that when God says He is going to come back and judge the world...guess what...He's going to come back and judge the world. When He says He wants all to be saved, He means it. He created the world in six days; I believe it. He flooded the whole world; I believe it. He sent His Son to die for my sins; I believe it.

I choose to believe all of it, regardless of what anyone else in the world says, because God has proven Himself to me as a result of my faith. With each passing day, my reliance upon His truth grows stronger and stronger. However, don't mistake what I am saying. God requires a faith commitment prior to this transformational work He will do in your life. We have to give up our pride and the arrogance fueled by the world before God is likely to do anything transforming in our lives.

The next logical step is growing in love. The very nature of God is what He wants to exist within you. This little thing called love is so vast we cannot fully comprehend it! For the one who has fully committed their life to God, who is fully reliant upon His Word of truth, each day will be a new lesson and experience in love.

This is the purpose of my testimony! My life shows the gospel at work, and it is a work in progress. I have remained fully committed to God. I have relied on His truth with every fiber of my being, and even amidst the ridicule of those who would attack my intellect for valuing Scripture above things like science.

Subsequently, I have been learning about real love every day since I made that commitment. I have learned about love in the context of marriage. I have learned about love through loss. I have learned about love through conflict. Love has taught me much when I was ill and dealing with pain. I have learned that love exists in the context of righteousness and judgment.

I am being daily changed from the inside out, to the point that if you put the thirty-three-year-old me side by side with the nineteen-year-old me, there would be a stark contrast in personality. The Radical Gospel changes people at a foundational and fundamental level. It is supposed to be such a mind-bending level of change that those of the world simply don't know how to deal with it or comprehend it. This is the gospel I've come to know and live.

The final call of the gospel is to endure until it is fully completed!

9

Pain Becomes a Reason for Joy

Count it all joy, my brothers, when you meet trials of various kinds, for you know that the testing of your faith produces steadfastness. And let steadfastness have its full effect, that you may be perfect and complete, lacking in nothing. (James 1:2–4)

Was James losing his mind here?! Take joy in trials? In suffering? This seems to go against any sort of logic. Much like my testimony while in China, what James seems to be highlighting here is learning to enjoy getting a beating, then doing it over again. To lack in nothing must mean that I can take a number of body blows and learn to love it, right?

I personally believe that a number of people jump off the bandwagon of Christianity when they realize that faith and suffering go hand in hand. Thus, we come back to the question of how pain and suffering could be a part of a good God's plan. One must personally answer this if they ever wish to have a real and engaging relationship with God.

In my testimonial experience with God, I have come to an answer that has brought me through pain, suffering, and despair. This answer is twofold: 1) Suffering exists where sin exists; and 2) part of a believer's life is not corrupted by sin.

Suffering Exists Where Sin Exists

If you have read the Bible to any extent, a common theme should be abundantly clear. Sin is the cause of all the bad we see in this world. It destroys and causes pain, and eventually it leads to death. Is sin God's fault? Absolutely not. It's mankind's fault. We are the reason for our own pain and suffering, not God. In our own arrogance and pride, we tend to view pain and suffering as things that are inherently evil. Therefore, a God who allows it must also be evil, or not fully good.

The truth of the matter, though, according to Scripture, is that pain is the result of sin and evil, not the origin of it. We hurt because something that is sinful and evil has already taken place. Sin entered the world as a result of mankind's will and choices. Therefore, God had to find a way to deal with it, and He did. As stated earlier in this book, Romans 8:3 tells us that "Jesus condemned sin in the flesh." Therefore, if our flesh is where sin dwells, then it makes full sense that our bodies will ache and slowly deconstruct, until they finally stop working and die. Does God really want this to happen?

Paul gives us the answer in Romans 7:13,

Did that which is good, then, bring death to me? By no means! It was sin, producing death in me through what is good, in order that sin might be shown to be sin, and through the commandment might become sinful beyond measure.

Remember that pain and suffering exist to show us what sin looks like, how it functions, and what its outcome is. It is like a red flag, letting us know what is going on inside of us.

Thus, in essence, pain and suffering in and of themselves are not bad things. We might even say they are good for us. They lead us to truth, which hopefully then leads us to God.

Now, for the believer, things are a bit different. Too many believers have this strange notion that having God in their lives means that they ought not to ever experience pain or suffering. Unfortunately for them, Scripture says quite the opposite:

> *If the world hates you, know that it has hated me before it hated you. If you were of the world, the world would love you as its own; but because you are not of the world, but I chose you out of the world, therefore the world hates you. Remember the word that I said to you: "A servant is not greater than his master." If they persecuted me, they will also persecute you. If they kept my word, they will also keep yours. But all these things they will do to you on account of my name, because they do not know him who sent me. If I had not come and spoken to them, they would not have been guilty of sin, but now they have no excuse for their sin. Whoever hates me hates my Father also* (John 15:18–23).

For believers, a part of us is no longer associated with the world, and the world simply doesn't know what to do with that. Therefore, we should expect things like persecution and suffering because we hold fast to the name of Jesus Christ as our God. In doing this, suffering actually becomes our ally, a testament to our faith in God. We become much like war heroes who return home to find a nation lifting them up due to the things that they have endured and accomplished on their country's behalf; so God sees us in our suffering similarly. Peter gives us more insight into this:

> *Beloved, do not be surprised at the fiery trial when it comes upon you to test you, as though something strange were happening to you. But rejoice insofar as you share Christ's sufferings, that you may also rejoice and be glad when his glory is revealed. If you are insulted for the name of Christ, you are blessed, because the Spirit of glory and of God rests upon you* (1 Pet. 4:12–14).

Peter has the audacity to suggest that any suffering that takes place within our relationship with God is actually worthy of causing joy because it means a heightened glory for the believer. We have in Christ a promise of true judgment, both good and bad, based upon what we have done on this earth and also what we have endured. So, we do not suffer for no good reason; when we suffer for the name of Christ, He will not let such a sacrifice go unnoticed.

This all comes back full circle to the flesh. The flesh is where sin dwells in your mortal person, and it is where death occurs. It is where pain manifests. Suffering abounds in the flesh. But none of these things affect the spirit that communes with God.

Part of a Believer's Life Is Not Corrupted by Sin

The spirit of a person who believes in God is not corrupted by sin. Therefore, pain and suffering does not exist within the spirit of a believer. I am fully aware that this may seem like mere semantics to people who wonder how we can differentiate between the flesh and the spirit. As a human being, it feels like both are part of one cohesive person, right? So, if I hurt in the flesh, then all of me will hurt. One cannot feel the flesh and feel the spirit in two different ways, can they? The experience of many people would probably say no. Yet the truth of Scripture would belt out a resounding yes!

The New Testament portion of the gospel message drives home the concept that to live by the spirit means to die to the flesh. We are constantly encouraged to walk by the spirit and not by the flesh. If anything, we see a call to separate the life we used to have in the flesh from the new life we now have in the Spirit. For "if anyone is in Christ He is a new creation; the old has passed away, behold the new has come" (2 Cor. 5:17).

What we certainly don't see coming out of a believer's spiritual life in Scripture is pain and suffering. This is vitally important because we actually have the ability to exist in the midst of sin, pain, and suffering, and yet our true life and personality can be far away from it, centered within our spirit. Remember, when we chose to unite with Christ, we also chose to die to the flesh. We divorced that part of us for good, and we ought not to go back. Therefore, we can exist in a body riddled with pain and suffering, and at the same time live in the spirit, where pain and suffering cannot touch us. That is where joy and peace and happiness dwell.

Don't forget this gem of wisdom:

> *So we do not lose heart. Though our outer self is wasting away, our inner self is being renewed day by day. For this light momentary affliction is preparing for us an eternal weight of glory beyond all comparison, as we look not to the things that are seen but to the things that are unseen.*

Pain Becomes a Reason for Joy

For the things that are seen are transient, but the things that are unseen are eternal (2 Cor. 4:16–18).

Once again, we see that although part of us is wasting away, another part of us is growing and thriving like never before. Which part are you choosing to focus on? Are you only looking to the things you can see, or are you choosing to dive into the realities of who you are that you cannot see? To dwell on the flesh is to dwell in pain, but to dwell in the spirit is life and peace regardless of the pain. Paul reminds us of that by saying,

For those who live according to the flesh set their minds on the things of the flesh, but those who live according to the Spirit set their minds on the things of the Spirit. For to set the mind on the flesh is death, but to set the mind on the Spirit is life and peace. For the mind that is set on the flesh is hostile to God, for it does not submit to God's law; indeed, it cannot. Those who are in the flesh cannot please God (Rom. 8:5–8).

When we dwell in the flesh, it's as if our whole life revolves around our mortal body. How many people do you see who spend countless hours at the gym to sculpt a body that will still eventually waste away? How many people do you know who practically live at the doctor's office because they want to be as healthy as possible? It's usually those same people who, when their bodies start to turn toward illness and death, become depressed and neurotic because their focus for so long had only been on the physical. Furthermore, I have never heard the argument of why a good God could allow pain and suffering, coming from a person who was not entirely focusing that argument on the flesh—the body.

What would happen if we began to focus in a greater degree on our spiritual life with Christ? I cannot speak dogmatically here, but my experience may lend some value. When I was sick and thought I was close to death, I reached the point where I finally gave up any hope for my body and put my full hope in my true life with Christ. The results were astounding. The pain didn't go away, but it seemed far less noticeable. Finding joy and peace was not difficult. In adopting the attitude that "if I die, then I die," I then put all my efforts into what Christ had put in my path, and there I found joy, joy, unspeakable joy.

A better description of this type of experience can be found in the writings of the famed French mathematician and theologian, Blaise Pascal. He was a young man when he died at the age of thirty-nine, and he suffered various health maladies throughout his life. Yet his brilliance was never diminished. That was due to one night in November 1654 when he had an experience with God that would change his view of living forever. This was his experience:

> The year of grace 1654, Monday, 23 November, feast of St. Clement, pope and martyr, and others in the martyrology. Vigil of St. Chrysogonus, martyr, and others. From about half past ten at night until about half past midnight, FIRE. GOD of Abraham, GOD of Isaac, GOD of Jacob not of the philosophers and of the learned. Certitude. Certitude. Feeling. Joy. Peace. GOD of Jesus Christ. My God and your God. Your GOD will be my God. Forgetfulness of the

world and of everything, except GOD. He is only found by the ways taught in the Gospel. Grandeur of the human soul. Righteous Father, the world has not known you, but I have known you. Joy, joy, joy, tears of joy.

I have departed from him: They have forsaken me, the fount of living water. My God, will you leave me? Let me not be separated from him forever. This is eternal life, that they know you, the one true God, and the one that you sent, Jesus Christ. Jesus Christ. Jesus Christ. I left him; I fled him, renounced, crucified. Let me never be separated from him. He is only kept securely by the ways taught in the Gospel: Renunciation, total and sweet. Complete submission to Jesus Christ and to my director. Eternally in joy for a day's exercise on the earth. May I not forget your words. Amen.

That night of fire fundamentally changed Pascal for the rest of his life. As other academics of the day would note, suffering became of little importance to him. It was as if he fully understood that the human body would indeed suffer at some point or another, so why should he waste any thought on it? Rather, he spent the remainder of his days in a very close relationship with Jesus Christ, which produced some of the most prominent theological writings in the world still to this day.

The experience of that night gave him such a real and radical revelation that he actually wrote down what had happened and then sewed the writing into his coat so that it would always be with him until the day he died.

Those last words, "Eternally in joy for a day's exercise on the earth," perfectly describes what the Christian believer can and should experience right now. A spirit-centered relationship with God is just that: spirit-centered. It is a life lived apart from the flesh and fully reliant upon the God who saves. When you have developed the practice of "forgetfulness of the world and everything, except God," then you will begin to really feel that "joy, joy, joy, tears of joy." Your sole focus on God will then render all other worldly circumstances as unimportant in comparison.

In this context, pain takes on a whole new meaning. It is no longer a point of depression and angst. Nor is it a reason to hate God. Rather, it becomes an opportunity that pushes us back into that spiritual focus. When things are going great, we so easily get caught up in the things of this world, but when things are not great, life comes down to two decisions: either focus on the bad or focus on God.

How To Lack in Nothing

Going back to the book of James, it makes much more sense. Consider it joy when those trials come because they aren't merely destroying you on the outside. Rather, they are actually helping to build up your spiritual life on the inside. The testing of your faith produces endurance, or steadfastness.

Another way of saying it is that practice makes permanent, and permanence leads to a fully complete result. As we encounter trials, we are offered yet another opportunity to turn to God and give Him 100 percent of our focus and attention. If we actually do that, then growth will always occur. Furthermore, we are training ourselves time and again to constantly turn to God in such a manner when the next trial comes. Each trial becomes easier and easier to deal with, until turning to God is simply second nature to us.

The truly mature Christian has a prime focus on God all the time and a peripheral view of the world. Even good times are always experienced in the context of a relationship with God. Consequently, bad times don't have near the effect because the mature believer is also still focused on God. This is how a believer can live and lack in nothing.

If you want to find someone who has highly developed this sort of faith, look to people who are on their deathbeds. Consider the ones who are the most comfortable with their circumstances and compare them to those people who are actually excited to die to this world and soon see Jesus. If you ask those people how they have the perspective they have, their answers will likely echo the truths in this chapter.

If the world keeps blaming God for pain and suffering, then the world will continue to be deceived. Pain apart from God is assuredly miserable and depressing, and certainly a by-product of sin and evil. Yet when God enters this scenario, suddenly what sin had hoped to be the ultimate result is rendered quite the opposite. God works all things together for good, for those who love Him and are called according to His purpose (Rom. 8:28).

In my own life, I have found arduous times of suffering to actually be the most rewarding in my relationship with God. When I felt as though I were close to death, my excitement about my life with God increased. Did I enjoy the pain? Not at all. But I did enjoy what God was faithfully doing through that pain. I fully enjoyed being built up and internally strengthened by the living God.

My life is living proof that what James conveyed, and what God has promised, really does work. Pain can lead to joy through the strengthening of your faith and through an ever-increasing endurance. If you want to lack in nothing in this life, then you must be prepared in the height of pain and suffering to hear from God, "My grace is sufficient for thee." If you are there and those words do not diminish your relationship with God one iota, then you have reached a complete and perfect faith endurance.

10

Illogical Man, Illogical God?

One of the biggest detriments to the Radical Gospel changing people's lives is the human intellect. For thousands of years now, humanity has struggled with the idea that their own mind, intelligence, and perception does them virtually no good when it comes to what God is offering to do within them. God even says that people need to have their minds transformed and renewed if they wish to grow closer to Him (Rom. 12:2). Yet the world has drawn the line in the sand around the human intellect. It has become the basis for any sort of authority on truth and reality.

In recent years, there has been a hyper-focus on things like facts, scholarly works, peer-reviewed material, logic and logical fallacies, education levels, and higher criticism. This world's system seems to proclaim:

- Educated people are smart.
- Smart people determine truth through study.
- Thousands of educated/smart people all disagree on what truth is.
- Therefore, uneducated people determine truth through whichever smart person agrees with their bias the most.

Is this not the way people are functioning in this day and age? Most people seem fine with a system like this until something serious comes up like climate change. Then, all of a sudden, people aren't allowed to think different things and consider them all to be truth. Someone has to be right and someone has to be wrong, and so another element to the system comes up called "peer review."

In simple terms, peer review takes place when multiple smart or educated people come together over a particular issue or research, and all agree on an aspect of it. They weigh and analyze the research based upon known facts, logic, and the overall depth of the research. These checks and balances in scholarship help to differentiate well-thought-out and well-researched ideas from poor scholarship.

So, the conclusion is that if all the smart people say one particular thing is correct, then it is pretty safe to say they are right. If no smart person says a particular view is correct, then it's probably not correct. But if there is a divide in views and various peer-reviewed groups of people are saying vastly different things on a particular subject, a cultural battle ensues. This is where we are at in the debates concerning climate change and evolution. This system has dominated academia for decades, and people are well accustomed to this form of thinking.

The primary problem with this system is that it doesn't take into account supernatural or spiritual things like God, sin, and salvation. It's not like we can put God or sin into a beaker, spray some chemicals on it, and conduct a test of our hypothesis. No, by definition, supernatural things do not follow the natural order of things, and therefore most people who work in this worldly system find a way to dismiss the

Illogical Man, Illogical God?

notion of a God. When it comes down to it, the peer-reviewed logic of man is far more supreme than an ancient history that suggests a God, says the wise worldly man.

Suppose, hypothetically, that all this supernatural stuff is real. According to Scripture, every human being has been corrupted with sin. How, then, can a corrupted person ever find real truth on their own initiative, using their own intellect? If we are all thoroughly corrupt, then something outside of the system must intervene to impart real truth that is uncorrupt. Do you see the problem here?

If God exists, then all of mankind must admit that we are all likely wrong about much of what we think. If God exists, then sin is real; and if sin is real, then we are all corrupt and incapable of coming to the truth on our own. Therefore, God must not exist! That is the only way the intellectual community remains an authority in our world. And yet I believe that God does exist because of my experience with Him. So, when I look at the world, I see a weird dynamic.

The world is similar to the plot of the movie *The Matrix*. Neo discovered that the world in which he lived was an illusion, that his true reality was that he and those around him were being used as batteries for machines, while being programmed to think they were living out a normal life. That is similar to my perception of the world today.

Many people are completely ignorant to the fact that there is a supernatural and spiritual component to their lives. They think that who they are is only made up of flesh and electrical impulses. They are completely unaware that they have a spirit that is dead to God. Sin is thriving in that spirit, and the only way people will become aware of it is to have an eye- and heart-opening experience, much like Neo had. The sad truth is that many have had that opportunity and still rejected it. Therefore, God has no qualms about letting them buy in to a delusion.

The Worldly Delusion

The coming of the lawless one is by the activity of Satan with all power and false signs and wonders, and with all wicked deception for those who are perishing, because they refused to love the truth and so be saved. Therefore God sends them a strong delusion, so that they may believe what is false, in order that all may be condemned who did not believe the truth but had pleasure in unrighteousness (1 Thess. 2:9–12).

There is no question that the maturation of sin over thousands of years has caused a worldly delusion. Why is it that all streams of education and scholasticism have increasingly moved away from God and the Bible as a true knowledge base? Not only have they stepped away, but now they actively mock those who even suggest that the truth of God is an option. It is a sad state of affairs when we can watch a chaotic world, full of violence and hate, search frantically for an answer that leads to peace, looking everywhere besides the Bible. In their minds and hearts, they have already determined that the answer cannot be found there. Why is this? Why do people dismiss such a viable option?

According to the Scripture above, this delusion has been sent by God, and the condemnation toward those who will not believe cannot be reversed. This tells us two sobering things. First, God's mercy and grace has limits, and there will come a time when God will no longer put up with unrighteous people, holding off judgment in the hopes that they might repent. Second, this delusion coincides with the already-saturated deception that the world is enduring. Therefore, the people of this world have very little hope of change for all sides are against the truth. However, their undoing is all their own fault; they partook in unrighteous living when they had the option to repent and follow God.

What we now see is an unusual, blatantly obvious bias against the Bible and God that virtually no other religion experiences. We don't see major scholastic institutions producing research and searching for evidence to disprove the Quran, the Baghivad Gita, or the Vedas. No, the Bible stands alone as the one major religious document that is repeatedly attacked in all areas of education, science, and philosophy. It's as if there is some draw, some attraction to hate and despise this particular book.

One general thought that has surfaced is the notion that Christians have caused this vitriol because of the seemingly archaic practices in the Bible, as well as their "hypocrisy." In essence, people in the world feel the need to bring believers low because biblical practices are so radically different from today's standards that modern people find them abhorrent and detestable, or because the Christian isn't even following what he says he believes. But even in this case, look at the alternative religions.

Radical Islamists can lop people's heads off, and even that does not bring the level of revolt that the Judeo/Christian Bible attracts. The same goes for the other religions and belief systems of the world. At some point, people will have to recognize that we are not on an even playing ground here. Something unusual makes people want to attack the Bible far more than any other religious text or practice, even when that religious text promotes violence. The Bible itself would call this a delusional practice, an active deception without the protection of a discerning, transformed mind. Delusional people buy in to the practice or movement without even thinking through the legitimacy of it all. But why would God allow this delusion to come upon people? Why would He cut off His mercy and grace from them?

> *Do not be deceived: God is not mocked, for whatever one sows, that will he also reap. For the one who sows to his own flesh will from the flesh reap corruption, but the one who sows to the Spirit will from the Spirit reap eternal life* (Gal. 6:7–8).

Do not forget that God is a righteous Judge! He will not allow unrighteousness to prevail. Therefore, those who have rejected Him their whole lives, instead enjoying fleshly, worldly, corrupt living, will not trick God in the end and accept Christ just as a formality to get into heaven. On the contrary! God sees the heart, and He knows which ones have this in mind. They will not succeed, for He will not be mocked. They are going to reap what they sow, and His method of achieving this is by sending a delusion so that they will not choose Him in an effort to be clever.

Unfortunately, those who live in a delusion have no clue that they are doing so. In fact, they often think they are far more intelligent and knowledgeable than those who are living in the Spirit. They have cast the narrative that the spiritual ones are "close-minded, ignorant, and unintellectual." Those who are spiritual are then forced to watch a train wreck in process as those who are deluded continue down the path of unrighteousness, even as they believe they are heading toward the pinnacle of life.

So, what are some examples of this deluded lifestyle? What are the tangible effects of this delusion?

1. Rejection of the created order: Gender identity and distorted human value

If you were to tell a person living a hundred years ago that progressive culture today would lead people to question whether they were a woman or a man, or perhaps some other made-up type of gender, you would have been considered mentally unstable. These sorts of realities ought to be easy to determine and obvious. Biology and design dictates gender. However, the intellect of modern humanity has found a way to rationalize these sorts of things.

An ethicist might wonder how we can live in a culture that will fight with fervor for the proper care and treatment of our earth, trees, and animals but also finds a way to rationalize the killing of unborn babies—and then have the audacity to call it health care. The same could be said for the newer movements of elder euthanasia that are becoming popular these days.

The value of human beings is under attack, and it seems incredibly peculiar that this can take place in a secular world that proposes the idea of survival of the fittest. In that context, humanity ought to band together in order to survive together, right? But what we see instead is humanity turning on each other at every opportunity. We find a way to diminish the inherent value of human beings who do not share our plans and goals.

Therefore, infants are disposable, and so are the elderly. Democrats probably wouldn't make too much of a fuss if Republicans were eradicated from the country, and vice versa. Black lives matter. Blue lives matter. Women are strong and independent and don't need oppressive men ruling their lives. White supremacy. Antifa. The list could go on and on. People are being devalued more and more each year, to the point that we devalue our own selves by not even recognizing our gender and biophysical makeup. The decay isn't just in politics or academia. It has eroded to the point of affecting very basic, commonsense things.

All of this is in contrast to one major view that deceived people cannot adopt: Humanity was designed with purpose and created by God for a reason. If that is the case, then there must be a designer, and if there is a designer, then it must be something supernatural like God. That changes things. If we are merely products of randomness, then human beings can be treated with frivolity. Who we are can be left up to the imagination. We can deal with inconveniences however we wish, even if it means killing other people. Every definable thing is up for debate because we make our reality.

However, from a biblical perspective, everything was designed and created with purpose and order. God made everything according to its kind. The sun, moon, and stars were developed for the signs and seasons, to govern the day and night. Plant life was made for food, etc. When it comes to gender, we see animal life created with the ability to mate and procreate. That screams of design. Humanity was made somewhat similar to animals, but we have very unique aspects to our created design. We were made in the image of God. We have the ability to invent, create, think abstractly, worship whatever or whoever we want, conduct complex problem solving, etc. No other animal is quite like us. We were designed for a purpose, and that purpose is a relationship with God Himself.

If a relationship with God exists, then there must also be a recognition of how God created the world, and for what purpose He designed things. Therefore, human value should be well understood. Human sexuality and gender should be obvious. The rest of creation should be a constant reinforcement to this way of thinking. Yet people today are questioning all of these things. Red flag number one is that even something as simple as gender has become something complex and confusing in many people's minds. The created order is now up for debate, and those people who are trying to unravel what is orderly truly do not know the living God. They have been blinded to truth. Many people live under this delusion today, and it gets worse.

2. Autonomy to the nth degree

"I make my own laws," says the so-called wise modern man. Another way of saying this is that *"your* truth can be *your* truth, and *my* truth can be *my* truth." As long as everyone remains tolerant of each other, we can all coexist in our own truths.

There is a strong value put on the notion that each of us can govern ourselves. The Bible describes it like this: "Everyone did what was right in their own eyes" (Jdgs. 21:25). When there is no universal lawgiver, then the development of universal laws falls on whoever is in the majority. And now we are back to peer-reviewed truth. As long as enough smart people declare it, it must be truth.

True autonomy is unsustainable, however, because if everyone made their own laws, we would soon see widespread anarchy. Instead, we have developed movements fueled by "experts" who tell us what truths we must believe. We then attach ourselves to that movement and follow it to whatever end it leads us to, including to what Francis Schaeffer referred to as the "moving consensus of men." Mankind determines truth for mankind because it is solely up to us to bring order out of the chaos of this world.

This kind of majority-fueled morality has led us to what we have today: a world full of division and chaos, with no true guiding principles. Autonomy has become man's pinnacle of existence. We want it our way. We want to dictate. We want convenience. We demand equality, but no one can agree on what it means to be equal. We cry out for justice, but what does justice really mean?

In the delusion of our autonomy, there is no standard and definable sense of right and wrong. If there is, that means there is a law apart from the one each individual makes for himself. That law would then be the standard. But with no definable sense of right and wrong, how can there be a standard of justice? How is equality even possible? This is where we find ourselves today.

Everyone has picked his or her own movement and group, and each person is fighting constantly for a bigger piece of the cultural pie. Everyone asks for an inch and wants a mile. Everyone has their own truth that will make all things better if only all the other people would simply agree. Meanwhile the rhetoric is ramping up, and the violence is increasing. In their autonomy, each group is depicting their counterparts as less than human.

Illogical Man, Illogical God?

The cruelest part of this delusion is that it is described with such a patriotic word—freedom. Freedom has become equated to autonomy. At one point in time, freedom meant to be released from bondage, to have one's shackles removed, to be treated with value as a human. However, that has all ceased. Freedom has now come to mean, "I get more, you give me more, and nothing ought to prevent me from doing what I want to do."

Throughout history, we have seen this autonomous ideology develop into what it is today, but one watershed moment opened the door to what we see happening now. On November 10, 1793, in Paris, France, the Notre Dame Cathedral was taken over by the new atheist cult of reason. A festival of reason was held with the altar of liberty at its center. Women dressed up as the Roman goddess Libertas and paraded around the cathedral. This defining moment during the French Revolution ushered in the notion that God is dead. In essence, the French people were declaring that they had been liberated from God and religion. Freedom existed fully apart from a deity, and the highest attainable value could now be found only in knowledge and reason.

Consequently, the leaders of the United States, which was forming itself as a nation about this time, were very much influenced by what was going on in France, as was most of the rest of Europe. The United States might have been founded on the principles of a Judeo-Christian ethic, but our actual belief from the beginning has been that mankind will prevail in this world with our work, intellect, invention, and reason. Supposedly freedom and liberty come through the application of these four things, but where is God in all of this? Where is the church? What we are seeing today was truly started over two hundred years ago. Autonomy has won the battle, and we even have a convenient idol now to commemorate man's autonomy: the Statue of Liberty (unsurprisingly, a gift from France).

The history of the United States is a testament to this ideology as it plays out. It started with a desire not to be oppressed by a king and a government across the ocean that was mandating taxes and imposing laws without any representation by the people who were being ruled. Today, however, we seek not to be oppressed by people who would use that evil word "no" toward us, or even worse, have the fortitude to disagree with our point of view and propose a quite opposite one. Likewise, our nation started out with people who were more than happy to work hard for every penny they got, knowing they had an equal say in how that money was used. Now people want to tell everyone else how their resources ought to be used without a dialogue, and handouts are often given to people unwilling to work. This autonomy without order or guiding principles has truly turned into an ugly beast. Very little of what freedom is today actually feels free.

Autonomy is culturally ingrained in our world today. It's not going anywhere unless something rips it out by the roots. Judging by what the rest of the world is doing, we're probably stuck with this ideology for a while.

3. Anthropocentric worship

A form of delusion that has been seeping into the church in the past few years has been an anthropocentric, man-centered worship. This is likely an end result of the prior two delusions. When autonomy rules, and when each individual revels in uninhibited expression, people tend to view the world as revolving around themselves. In that context, how they feel and think and perceive is of the utmost importance to their reality. Therefore, within the church we see worship becoming more and more an act that has as its primary function making people feel what they want to feel. God becomes more real to them when they feel those shivers down their spine, and a melody touches their souls and brings tears to their eyes.

People flock to those churches that have a professional band, amazing stage equipment, and everything needed to set the mood so that people can feel those goose bumps during *their* worship time. Contrary to this, fewer and fewer people faithfully attend a church where everyone stands and sings a-cappella from a hymnbook. The feeling there just isn't the same. A common complaint I hear these days is, "I just don't feel the Spirit in this place."

This mind-set actually has the opposite effect from what everyone thinks it is having. The more we seek out worship for our own feelings, the less and less God is involved in the act altogether. After a while, this practice will lead us to church hopping. When we become tired of the current worship style, and we are not feeling what we want to feel, it's time for a new church. Soon church hopping becomes old, and we start to wonder why we even need a church to worship in anyhow. At that point, God is no longer even in the peripheral view of the act of worship; He's gone altogether.

The great deception in worship is that it is meant to benefit the human person. It's not! The object of worship is God Himself, and the word for "worship," *avodah*, has the same Hebrew root from which we get the word "work." In essence, our worship is what we give to God for His blessing and benefit. It is our energy, effort, and work given to Him through song, money, service, sacrifice, and beyond, which ultimately blesses the Lord and recognizes His glory. Nowhere in this do we see the benefit of the worshiper as a primary outcome of the worship.

Now, it's not like worship hasn't been exploited in times past. Remember, Jesus created a whip and drove people out of the temple because they were ultimately exploiting worship. Likewise, the Catholic Church helped to spur on the Protestant reformation because it was selling indulgences to pay for wars by promising people less time in purgatory. Worship had become something used for the purpose of the worshipers instead of something offered to God. History has shown that when worship has degraded to that level, it usually precedes a major upheaval within the body of faith.

Man-centered worship is like an autoimmune disease. Once it starts, nothing is going to stop it. Nothing is going to prevent its course in the body unless severe measures are taken. Instead, the best we can hope for is to manage it until there is a drastic change. The worship practices of today are lulling people to sleep instead of waking them up to the truth and the practice of spiritual living. It's subtle enough to make people think they are doing great, but the telltale sign is that they don't ever grow or change. They use their worship time as a crutch to get them through the week, instead of using the faith building of the week to motivate their genuine worship in the body of believers.

Ultimately, if you are experiencing no growth, you're doing something wrong. And no, growth is not indicated by reading the latest Christian self-help book, then posting on social media that you have been forever changed by it. We're talking radical growth here. Dying to the old self and living in the new Spirit. Praying without ceasing. Fasting. Sacrificing. Really transforming your mind. Cultivating a new personality. Learning new things about love and participating in that love. Ultimately, such radical growth leads to one faith conclusion. No longer do you care about your physical existence on this earth because your true existence is with Christ. At that point, your worship reflects where your true life is, where your true home is.

Thus, all of our worship ought to be directed toward the Father and offered to the Father, as we ought to be people who understand and thrive in the truth. The Scripture says, "...true worshipers will worship the Father in spirit and truth, for the Father is seeking such people to worship him" (John 4:23). This is further confirmation that if we allow any part of our flesh, mind, or emotions to work their way into what worship means for us, we have stopped worshiping in the spirit. If we worship in any ways that are contrary to the truth, then we have maligned the object of our worship.

Our delusional world communicates the message to us that says all good things must be tangibly beneficial to mankind or else they are not good. Yet the counterintuitive nature of God says that worship is the sacrifice of our benefits in order to give God glory. In that sacrifice, we see the most beneficial results, though they are not necessarily tangible (Rom. 12:1–2).

Where Does True Logic Exist?

In our intellect-heavy environment, one question truly needs to be asked and answered: Does mankind even have the capacity to truly be logical? Yes, I know that we have made up all of these systems, and methods, and logical fallacies. But at the root of all of it is sin. We are thoroughly corrupt, despite our efforts to think our way to goodness and justice.

This logical method has attacked the validity of Scripture, suggesting that supernatural things do not really exist, and ultimately that there is no God. Of course, Scripture has a few things to say about this:

> *The fool says in his heart, "There is no God." They are corrupt, they do abominable deeds; there is none who does good. The Lord looks down from heaven on the children of man, to see if there are any who understand, who seek after God (Psa. 14:1–2).*

> *For the word of the cross is folly to those who are perishing, but to us who are being saved it is the power of God. For it is written, "I will destroy the wisdom of the wise, and the discernment of the discerning I will thwart."*
> *Where is the one who is wise? Where is the scribe? Where is the debater of this age? Has not God made foolish the wisdom of the world? For since, in the wisdom of God, the world did not know God through wisdom, it pleased God through the folly of what we preach to save those who believe. For Jews demand signs and Greeks seek wisdom, but we preach Christ crucified, a stumbling block to Jews and folly to Gentiles, but to those who are called, both Jews and Greeks, Christ the power of God and the wisdom of God.*
> *For the foolishness of God is wiser than men, and the*

Illogical Man, Illogical God?

weakness of God is stronger than men. For consider your calling, brothers: not many of you were wise according to worldly standards, not many were powerful, not many were of noble birth. But God chose what is foolish in the world to shame the wise; God chose what is weak in the world to shame the strong (1 Cor. 1:18–27).

Logic defined is: "reasoning conducted or assessed according to strict principles of validity." The truth of logic is that reasoning and assessment do not come before knowledge and wisdom. They are by-products of knowledge and wisdom. Likewise, principles of validity are extrapolated from presupposed knowledge. Therefore, logic is a construct of human thought, developed from whatever well of knowledge and wisdom we draw from.

Thus, the Jewish logic was to seek out signs, and the Greek logic was to seek further wisdom. But God threw a wrench into the whole system of the world by doing something that made no sense to the world's logic, wisdom, or knowledge. The almighty God saved His people, and brought the opportunity of salvation to the world by Himself dying like a criminal on a cross. He took uneducated fishermen and made them His closest disciples. He started His kingdom in this world by dying, then leaving it to poor, uneducated men to go around the world and advance the kingdom. Why would almighty God do it this way? It makes no sense from the world's logic.

God certainly does not follow our principles of validity. From the creation account in which the world was made in six days, to the sun stopping in the sky, to the Red Sea parting, to an angel striking down 185,000 Assyrian soldiers, to a donkey speaking to a prophet, to a king behaving like a wild animal for seven years, to ravenous lions calming in Daniel's presence, to three friends walking through a fiery furnace without even smelling of smoke, to water turned into wine, to over five thousand people being fed with just five loaves of bread and two fish, to God Himself ultimately dying on a cross and then rising from the dead shortly after, the entire story of God is riddled with things that make no logical sense to a world that is trying to think and reason apart from God.

In doing it this way, God has forced people to make a decision right out of the gate: "Do I believe it, or do I not believe it?" He has constructed it so that we must choose to believe a God who has shown us many logical things, like the creation all around us, but also many illogical things. If God is almighty, then those illogical things must also be truth. He gives us only one real option here: If God, then…?

If God exists, and I believe in that, then:

1. I must believe in who He is: an all-powerful, all-knowing, infinite, and eternal God.

2. I must believe in what He has done, even illogical miracles and the creation of the world.

3. I must believe His message, found in the Bible, to be supernaturally inspired.

4. I must believe His interaction with humanity is real.

In other words, if God, then everything His Word says is true and accurate, and I must put my faith in it. On the other end of things, some people will choose not to believe in God.

Of course, God would consider them to be fools, but I wouldn't expect them to think anything other than that believers of God are illogical, unintellectual, borderline-crazy cultists. If God doesn't exist, then honestly, that is how all devoted believers would seem.

So, unbelievers can continue to enjoy the hedonistic lifestyle of "eat, drink, and be merry," saturating themselves with the logic of the world and being thoroughly offended and disgusted whenever a believer disagrees with them. To them, God doesn't exist, and neither does sin or the consequences of sin. Which one is correct, and which one is wrong? Each side will think the other is wrong, but time will tell.

The world believes that true knowledge and logic exists in man's formulated, peer-reviewed thinking and research, which brings about conclusions and change. I believe that God is the Source of all true logic, knowledge, and wisdom.

Believers of God, Learning from the World

What makes no sense in all of this are the believers who still use the world's form of logic and reasoning to determine truth. We see this in many forms: the overemphasis of science compared to historical Scripture; the intertwining of the culture of progressivism; the over-loyal adherence to logical fallacies, peer reviews, and expert-driven facts. It's as if people who profess to believe in God aren't quite sure if God is really almighty or not. They like the idea of God, but they don't fully buy in to the notion that He is an all-powerful, all-knowing Being, who defies much of this worldly logic. They have trouble really believing in the supernatural. Therefore, they must hold on to those things they think make sense.

So, these "believers" challenge everything to the hilt. they say that God's creation didn't really happen the way it was presented in Scripture. Adam and Eve weren't real people; that whole part of the narrative was some strange form of Hebrew poetry that proves it was just a mythological story. The account of Jonah isn't real because I can't believe in a big fish swallowing a person and then spitting him back out alive. Job wasn't real because then we would have to believe that God makes deals with Satan. There was no worldwide flood; there's simply not enough water to cover the mountain peaks. People never lived to be over nine hundred years old. Anything and everything that doesn't make sense to a modern world's logical standard must be eradicated from our thinking.

The problem with going down that road is that eventually you will get to Jesus. If you can't believe in Adam and Eve, or Jonah, or Job, or a worldwide flood, then how in the world are you going to believe that a man, who is also God, was killed on a cross and came back to life days later? Likewise, if you can't believe in the reality of these things, how do you deal with Jesus referencing them as if they were real, or Paul, or Peter? How do you deal with Romans 5, which says that sin came through one man, Adam, and was dealt with by the one Man, Christ? This becomes a big mess for those who cannot accept the seemingly illogical claims of Scripture and the supernatural phenomena of God.

Believers cannot continue down this road! Things are quickly going to come down to a staunch choice: Either you believe God or you don't. Either the Bible is entirely true and depicting real things, or it's not. To be wishy-washy about it is to be just like the "double-minded man, unstable in all his ways" (James 1:8). He asked for wisdom from God, but he doubted in that wisdom. Scripture says that he ought not to think God will give him any wisdom at that point because his faith is lacking. The church today is made up of many people like this. Unwilling to believe in what is unexplainable and doubtful of God, they profess belief, but they live like the world.

Illogical Man, or Illogical God?

What is more illogical? Believing that there is a God who exists, or that mankind has the capacity to logically come up with the way to success and peace and bring order out of chaos? For those who think the idea of an existent God is more illogical, my question to you is, What do you make of the world, then? Our world seems to be getting worse and worse with each passing year. Chaos is abounding more and more. We have never had more information and knowledge than we do today, right at our fingertips. Yet, all we see is a less-educated, more ignorant, far more hostile world than ever before.

In the twentieth century alone, more people were murdered than in the previous nineteen centuries combined. If anything, we can say one thing with confidence: Humanism and logic apart from God and religion has certainly not led to peace. Man's logic is not working. It's having the opposite effect from what it is supposed to have.

Mankind has bought a deception, hook, line, and sinker. It started with the suppression of the truth of creation and the created order, which put sufficient doubt in people's minds. Through speculation, they began to adopt the notion that the end of all being must be the happiness of man.

Therefore, autonomy began to reign supreme in the minds and hearts of humanity, and everyone began to progressively reach out for just one more ounce of freedom. Due to a mind-set of autonomy, people of faith began to incorporate it into their religious practices, soon developing a man-centered form of worship.

All of this has been slowly and methodically playing out for decades, even hundreds of years, until what we see now is a general populace so concerned with all aspects of freedom and autonomy that the only God that exists for them is one who serves man and contributes to his happiness. This deception is protected by the barrier of science, academia, and scholarship. Ultimately, man's logic is the measure by which any truth claim is now weighed, and it is found wanting if the claim asserts the existence of a God that is not subservient to man. God must be exactly what is beneficial to man, and that alone, or else that God is worthless and pointless.

However, the God of Scripture claims complete sovereignty. He stands alone above all other creation as a supreme being. What He says is what happens. His plan and will for this world will come to fruition, whether we like it or not. By His standard and logic, everything will come to a culmination at the end time. God allows evil for a time for the sake of His plan on this earth. He is always in complete control! But God shows truth through our experiences, and our experiences reveal mysteries to us.

God has set up our existence through a series of mysteries that mankind cannot fully know or understand until we put our trust in Him and experience it firsthand. This kills man's logic where it stands because God goes so far beyond what makes any sense to us, we must simply be content with trusting in Him. From my perspective, the result of man's logic has been painfully apparent. The only real positive change I've experienced in life took place when God moved and worked; it was unexplainable but very real. I fully yield my logic for the sake of God's supernatural plan.

11

How To Discern Truth through the Mysteries of God

Ah, yes, the mysteries of God. This may sound cryptic and somewhat hokey, but the Bible actually uses the term "mysteries" quite often. The base meaning of the word mystery is "something hidden now to be revealed at a later time." These mysteries are the very things that help people to step through the darkness and into the light, but none of them come by way of logic or reason. They come by way of trust and faith.

To give credibility to this idea of God's mysteries, the apostle Paul states clearly: "This is how one should regard us, as servants of Christ and stewards of the mysteries of God" (1 Cor. 4:1). Furthermore, Paul goes on to say that,

> *In him we have redemption through his blood, the forgiveness of our trespasses, according to the riches of his grace, which he lavished upon us, in all wisdom and insight making known to us the mystery of his will, according to his purpose, which he set forth in Christ* (Eph. 1:7–9).

The mysteries of God are numerous, even to the point that the entire plan of God on this earth and during this age is still largely a mystery to us. We don't yet know how or when all the things described in Scripture will transpire. We certainly don't know the full extent of what will happen when we stand before God and are judged. Likewise, we don't know what the restored earth and new bodies will really be like. All we can do is imagine those things based upon the few nuggets of revelation given to us in the Scriptures, but realistically, they are still under a shroud of mystery.

However, some mysteries exist that are not future plans of God that we must wait to find out about. These mysteries become revealed as we enter a relationship with Christ and begin to act according to His Word. Through these types of revelations, people can understand the truth that goes far beyond logic and reason. In other words, God is not going to let people analyze their way to a spirit-building, soul-transforming truth. They must walk with God through experience for that truth to really have meaning and application.

For example, there are multiple things described in Scripture that we can do today that will reveal mysterious truths in our lives and make them active. The first of these mysteries, and probably the most important, is the fear of the Lord.

Fearing the Lord

The entire concept of fearing the Lord has made many modern Christians uneasy and confused. Are we supposed to be afraid of God? To fear a God who supposedly loves us and cares about us? It doesn't make much sense. Once again, God presents a seemingly contradictory and illogical premise, that a God who loves us should also be feared by us. People don't know what to do with that idea, and so they say things like,

"It must be an awe-like fear," more like a type of respect. They begin to rationalize what this term could mean based upon the God they have formulated in their minds.

However, when we look to the original language used, rationalization becomes less of an option. The Hebrew word *yare* has a base meaning of "fear, to be afraid, and terror." Likewise, the Greek word for "fear," *phobos*, has a base meaning of "fear, terror, reverence." One thing is sure: This fear may be reverent, but that reverence is not separated from terror or fear. It's all part of the same idea. There is a part of us that should be afraid of God, fearful of Him. But what does that fear look like?

The Bible describes some key things that should put a healthy fear within each one of us: "And do not fear those who kill the body but cannot kill the soul. Rather fear him who can destroy both soul and body in hell" (Matt. 10:28).

Just imagine for a moment that you began by existing and having a distinct personality, good friends and family, a meaningful job, a skillset and talents, hopes and desires, and everything else that comes from being a human in this world. All of that is active in your life, and then, in one moment, by one word, everything that you are is now destroyed and dismantled. You might as well have never existed.

God has the power to do that with little effort on His part. I don't know about you, but the thought that He has the power to make me as though I never existed puts shivers of fear down my spine. Is the fear of the Lord an issue of respect? Absolutely! But respect in this context still requires a bit of terror-like fear. Does this mean that God wishes for people to only feel that sort of fear around Him? Not at all. A few verses later, we read this encouragement:

How To Discern Truth through the Mysteries of God

Fear not, therefore; you are of more value than many sparrows. So everyone who acknowledges me before men, I also will acknowledge before my Father who is in heaven, but whoever denies me before men, I also will deny before my Father who is in heaven (Matt. 10:31–33).

In one moment, we are encouraged to fear God because of His sheer power to destroy us. Yet a few verses later, we see the encouragement to "fear not" because God sees much value in us and will respond to our relational acknowledgment of Jesus. This is a paradox we see in our relationship with God because how do we fear and not fear at the same time? God is serious and loving, judging and also merciful, and it seems illogical that He wants a relationship with us that involves us both fearing Him and not fearing Him.

The only real example I can think of in this life was my relationship with my father when I was a young child. During those days, I always had a healthy, underlying fear of him. My father had an immense amount of power compared to me, and when I did something wrong and punishment was imminent, there was always a fear of what he could or would do to punish me. At the same time, however, I loved my father and I knew that he loved me. There was absolutely no question that my father had my best interests in mind, and yet that fear remained. It remained until I reached an age when I knew my power, strength, and ability matched his. At that point, I didn't fear him anymore, but I certainly still loved him. However, he ceased being a father then (in a parenting sort of sense), and he became more of an encourager and supporter as I went out on my own.

The primary difference between my father and God the

Father is that God will always be our parent. Scripture says that we are His sons and daughters, adopted into His family. We will never reach an equivalent level of power to Him, so there remains the necessity for fear, a healthy fear, a fear that says, "God doesn't mess around."

Scripture gives us a little more insight into this God who doesn't mess around:

The Son of Man goes as it is written of him, but woe to that man by whom the Son of Man is betrayed! It would have been better for that man if he had not been born (Matt. 26:24).

But whoever causes one of these little ones who believe in me to sin, it would be better for him to have a great millstone fastened around his neck and to be drowned in the depth of the sea (Matt. 18:6).

When God starts using phrases like "it would have been better for that man had he not been born," it is safe to say that what God can do to us should bring a certain level of fear. Likewise, for those who cause little ones to sin, it would be better for them to have a great millstone fastened to their neck and be thrown to the bottom of the sea. God shows that when we cross the line with Him, the outcome is going to be bad beyond what we can imagine. It just may be that there will come a day when those who mocked God may wish they had never been born. This type of experience is not out of the realm of scriptural possibility.

On the other hand, fearing God does not just connote a negative thing. Being afraid of God doesn't mean that bad things are imminent. On the contrary, the fear of the Lord is the beginning of much good, and therein lies the mystery of it. First and foremost, the fear of the Lord is our starting point for a relationship with Him:

The fear of the Lord is the beginning of knowledge; fools despise wisdom and instruction (Proverbs 1:7).

The fear of the Lord is hatred of evil. Pride and arrogance and the way of evil and perverted speech I hate (Proverbs 8:13).

The fear of the Lord is the beginning of wisdom, and the knowledge of the Holy One is insight (Proverbs 9:10).

The fear of the Lord prolongs life, but the years of the wicked will be short (Proverbs 10:27).

In the fear of the Lord one has strong confidence, and his children will have a refuge (Proverbs 14:26).

The fear of the Lord is a fountain of life, that one may turn away from the snares of death (Proverbs 14:27).

The fear of the Lord is instruction in wisdom, and humility comes before honor (Proverbs 15:33).

The fear of the Lord leads to life, and whoever has it rests satisfied; he will not be visited by harm (Proverbs 19:23).

The reward for humility and fear of the Lord is riches and honor and life (Proverbs 22:4).

When studying the book of Proverbs, we see that the fear of the Lord is quite diverse. It is where knowledge begins, as well as wisdom. Fearing God actually produces instruction in wisdom. Fearing God correlates to the hatred of evil. It leads to life and prolongs life. It instills confidence and provides rest and a refuge. And the reward of it is riches, honor, and life. This is the mystery! It is laid out right before us, but no one can truly understand it until they have experienced the results.

Those who do not fear God will not produce true knowledge or wisdom; at the very least, they will be indifferent about evil. It doesn't matter if they have had years of education. Without the fear of the Lord, all they will produce is pseudo-knowledge and pseudo-wisdom, and these things will lead people away from life and good things. They will walk in their delusion straight toward a death-full existence.

However, when we embrace the fear of the Lord, the mystery will be revealed and the blinders will be taken away from our eyes. Life will become simpler. Knowledge and wisdom will be properly interpreted and applied. The hand of God will guide our lives and build us up for good things. All of this will be easily seen and understood, and it will feel strange that other people cannot see what we can see.

This is the essence of the mystery of fearing God. People who mock God will likely continue to mock God and His followers because they can't see and understand what believers experience, and they think it is ludicrous that they cannot experience what believers experience. Therefore, they discount the whole thing. The mystery has not been revealed to them, and God, in His brilliance, set it all up that way.

The very best lesson taught on fearing God comes from Psalm 34:

> *This poor man cried, and the Lord heard him and saved him out of all his troubles. The angel of the Lord encamps around those who fear him, and delivers them. Oh, taste and see that the Lord is good! Blessed is the man who takes refuge in him! Oh, fear the Lord, you his saints, for those who fear him have no lack! The young lions suffer want and hunger; but those who seek the Lord lack no good thing. Come, O children, listen to me; I will teach you the fear of the Lord. What man is there who desires life and loves many days, that he may see good? Keep your tongue from evil and your lips from speaking deceit. Turn away from evil and do good; seek peace and pursue it. The eyes of the Lord are toward the righteous and his ears toward their cry. The face of the Lord is against those who do evil, to cut off the memory of them from the earth. When the righteous cry for help, the Lord hears and delivers them out of all their troubles. The Lord is near to the brokenhearted and saves the crushed in spirit* (Psa. 34:6–18).

The fear of the Lord starts with humility: "This poor man cried, and the Lord heard him and saved him." It then moves to experience: "The angel of the Lord encamps around those who fear him.... Oh, taste and see that the Lord is good." Then comes an exhortation: "Oh fear the Lord, you his saints, for those who fear him have no lack.... Those who seek the Lord lack no good thing."

At this point, the author blatantly says, "I will teach you the fear of the Lord." The key components of the fear of the

Lord are as follows:

1. Keep your tongue from evil, and your lips from speaking deceit.
2. Turn away from evil and do good.
3. Seek peace and pursue it.
4. Live in righteousness, and you will have the Lord's attention; He will hear you.
5. God will respond to the righteous person's cry for help.

When we participate in these five activities, we are reflecting the fear of the Lord in us. If we fear God, we will watch what we say and not deceive people. Our constant task will be turning away from evil in order to do good. Our desire will be to go after peace. Our state of being will be righteousness, and we will not be too proud to cry out to God for help. When these things are present in us, we do, indeed, fear God.

The mystery of fearing God is presented all throughout Scripture, and it is even found within the history of the church. Fearing God is one of the key things that led to successful church growth. Consider Acts 9:31:

> *So the church throughout all Judea and Galilee and Samaria had peace and was being built up. And walking in the fear of the Lord and in the comfort of the Holy Spirit, it multiplied.*

The church drastically multiplied over those first years as the apostles carried the message of truth to new towns and people who hadn't heard the gospel. However, this verse especially shares two key things that helped the church develop rapidly: walking in the fear of the Lord and the comfort of the Holy Spirit. These things were vital for church growth, and they are still vital to this day.

The primary problem with fearing God in the modern twenty-first century world is that most people don't feel the need to fear God. God is a good, moral protagonist, but to them He is not real. He is a great idea, thought, or disposition, but He is not real. The events of Scripture are so far removed with so much distance in time from our modern day and the spiritual awareness of the people today, they simply don't see God as a real being. They see Him as a storybook character.

Of course, for those same reasons, I don't fear Zeus. I don't fear the Roman god Jupiter. I don't fear Brahma or Vishnu. These gods are fictitious renditions of perhaps some supernatural phenomena, but they are truly made-up beings. There is no historical account of their dealings on this earth. There is zero evidence for their reality.

In contrast, the God of the Bible is real. A real Being. A Being who has been involved in human history. A mountain of evidence shows His reality. A real God should be respectfully feared. A make-believe god should not be feared. Those who do not fear God either don't know what His Word actually says, or they don't believe He is real. There is no gray area in this.

So, what fearing God does so well is weed out the fakers from the true believers. Those who fear God with all their being discover the mystery revealed of His knowledge and wisdom, which are truth. We cannot adequately know the truth without first having the fear of the Lord.

The Mystery of Being a Living Sacrifice

The second mystery involves the peculiar calling for all believers to be a living sacrifice (Rom. 12:1). The words living and sacrifice simply ought not to go together, right? A sacrifice is a thing that is dead or lost. You sacrifice your time by losing it to something. You sacrifice your money, and it's gone out of your wallet. The sacrifice of a body connotes a death that must have occurred. How can we be alive and a sacrifice at the same time? Furthermore, why would it even be good to be a living sacrifice? Why should a person think something that sounds like such an unpleasant process is beneficial?

To compound this whole mess, Romans 12:1 uses another counterintuitive phrase:

> *I appeal to you therefore, brothers, by the mercies of God, to present your bodies as a living sacrifice, holy and acceptable to God, which is your spiritual worship.*

The term "spiritual worship" is actually written in the Greek as *logiken latreian*, which is literally "rational (logical) service." So God is basically saying that in light of the fact that He exists and that He set up the process of salvation for you and me (well-explained in Romans 1–11), the next logical thing we can do to serve God is to present our bodies as living sacrifices. How like God to say such a thing! He tells us that something that seems illogical at first sight is actually the most logical thing we can do!

So, what does it look like to be a living sacrifice? Imagine, much like an animal sacrifice would be, you are lying on the brazen altar before God. God is looking down at you as He

How To Discern Truth through the Mysteries of God

says, "I want this part of you for this particular purpose." In that moment, there is no discussion, no complaining, no overthinking the situation. Your body is no longer yours; it is God's. When He says, "You are going to give Me this part of you right now," there isn't even a need for dialogue because you already gave up that right to God when you surrendered your life to Him. Therefore, a true believer has already given up his body for the sake of Christ.

What God does with such a sacrifice is to develop a wholly new person from the inside out: true life, true growth, and an abundance of good things. This is what living for God and being a sacrifice at the same time looks like. God is taking more of this physical world's draw away from you and instilling more spiritual life within you. In this process, the mystery of true living and true life are revealed.

However, God never takes away our free will in all of this. People still have a choice. When God asks you to sacrifice part of your physical existence for His sake, a believer can still say no, and, in fact, many do. However, in saying no, we are not simply rejecting the act that God is trying to do. We are rejecting God Himself. Why would any believer say no to God? People can get too attached to the materialistic things of this life and find themselves unable to let go of their hold over them. As was the case in the parable of the rich young ruler, we see this struggle play out:

> *And behold, a man came up to him, saying, "Teacher, what good deed must I do to have eternal life?" And he said to him, "Why do you ask me about what is good? There is only one who is good. If you would enter life, keep the commandments." He said to him, "Which ones?" And*

Jesus said, "You shall not murder, You shall not commit adultery, You shall not steal, You shall not bear false witness, Honor your father and mother, and, You shall love your neighbor as yourself." The young man said to him, "All these I have kept. What do I still lack?" Jesus said to him, "If you would be perfect, go, sell what you possess and give to the poor, and you will have treasure in heaven; and come, follow me." When the young man heard this he went away sorrowful, for he had great possessions (Matt. 19:16–22).

Jesus required this young ruler to be a true, living sacrifice for God. When it came down to that one thing—in this case, his riches—he could not make that sacrifice. The allure of his physical existence pulled him away from God, and he left sorrowful. In the same way, many Christian believers have that one thing, or perhaps multiple things, they are unwilling to give up in this physical life. This is where the mystery of being a living sacrifice blinds those who have not seen what it actually does to a person.

When we give up all our rights of control over our own bodies and all the other physical things we possess, nothing stands in the way of our spiritual life with God. In other words, true prosperity comes from giving up everything to God and allowing Him to make your life good. No longer is truth hindered by the temptation of this world; rather, in being a living sacrifice and putting our full reliance upon God, the truth becomes abundantly clear and without competition from the deception of sin.

Therefore, the one who walks out his days constantly sacrificing himself according to what God says is the one who lives vibrantly like few others ever live. This mystery is not exclusive, nor is it difficult, but it is far more thought of than applied, doubted, or left untried.

This all comes back full circle to the object of worship. If God exists and is truly the One whom we worship through our sacrificial giving, then why are people struggling with truly being a living sacrifice? The truth is, people don't view God as more important than themselves in worship because they are more concerned about how they feel and less concerned about what they are giving to God.

The Mystery of True Freedom

Galatians 5:1 tells us that "For freedom, Christ set us free, stand firm therefore and do not submit again to a yoke of slavery." Freedom is absolutely part of what it means to live for God. Christ's plan for us is to be sufficiently free from bondage. However, freedom is not at all what we have made it out to be. In the modern man's mind, freedom or liberty is equative to autonomy. To man, freedom happens when he makes his own laws, creates his own rules, and lives unhindered in his ability to express himself however he wishes. This is the ideal of freedom in our modern culture.

However, Scripture depicts a much different type of freedom. Romans 8:20–21 says,

> *For the creation was subjected to futility, not willingly, but because of him who subjected it, in hope that the creation itself will be set free from its bondage to corruption and obtain the freedom of the glory of the children of God.*

Two very important things are being communicated here. First, the essence of freedom is a release from bondage to corruption. Freedom is not being released from any and all types of bondage.

Some bondage is a good thing. Civilizations that thrive are bound to a common law of conduct. In other words, the law holds them in some form of bondage, or accountability, for the sake of everyone else. There is nothing wrong with that kind of bondage. The key word here is corruption. Bondage to corruption is the true problem. Therefore, true freedom comes about when creation is no longer bound to any corruption. Christ has set us free to escape corruption.

The second part to this is that freedom and glory function in a mystery together. For a person to truly be free, he must have an understanding, an appreciation, and the practice of glory. The freedom of the glory of the children of God suggests that those who have fully committed to God, and who have been brought into a state of glory as the children of God, will experience the by-product of true freedom. This is a mystery because no one will truly understand freedom until they have experienced this whole process.

The Glory Problem

Our world has a massive glory problem! Not only do most people not know what glory means, but many have also tweaked the definition. In our modern day, glory is thought of as a reputation, a legacy, and renown. Because of what we have done, we receive a certain amount of glory. Therefore, people who have achieved much in areas of renown are looked at as having immense glory. Some prime examples of this include sports stars, famous musicians, and perhaps military and world leaders. In the sight of man, these people all have glory. They are idolized and romanticized into some mythical level of ability they likely never actually had.

Corrupt humanity does not have nearly the level of glory that is projected onto them. Every person is still human, still decaying, and still far from perfect, yet the masses flock around these specific "heroes" and treat them as though they are something far bigger than a mortal, corrupt human. They do this because mankind puts the center of glory within themselves. The reason we project glory onto others is to give us hope that perhaps mankind might become something beyond mortal on our own initiative. Everything starts and ends with humanity, and thus, this way of thinking has come to be called humanism.

The cycle of sin plays out well in this framework. People suppress the truth and begin to speculate about man-centered truth. Their hearts begin to darken, and they become arrogant and prideful. Instead of viewing the Creator as the pinnacle of existence and giving Him glory, they view man as the pinnacle of existence and mankind then glorifies mankind. The end result of all of this is that people will worship the creation rather than the Creator.

Remember now what glory means. As I mentioned in an earlier chapter, "glory" comes from the Hebrew word *kavad*, which literally means "to be heavy." Therefore, to have glory is to be more weighty than someone or something else, to have more clout. Thus, when God says in Scripture that He will get the glory, He is saying He will prove He has more power than the ones with whom He is dealing. No one is going to outpower God. So, can man truly have glory?

Man's problem with glory is that on our own initiative, glory stops with death. We can have a limited glory, up until the point when we stare death in the face—and then death always wins. Mankind does not have glory over death, so does mankind have a glory worth striving for? Our corruptness destroys any glory we thought we had. For a time, Michael Jordan might be considered the greatest basketball player ever, but he is not so great that he's going to beat death. His glory only exists where his power lies, and that power is insignificant when looking at the entirety of life. Eventually his legacy will be forgotten or taken over by an up-and-coming star. Is that the kind of glory we really want?

However, when God intervenes, real glory becomes possible. When the gospel begins to work in a person's life and he is changed from the inside out, death is one of the things that is beaten. With death destroyed and believers brought into the family of God as children, those children will reflect God's glory in their lives. Nothing will overpower us, just like nothing will overpower God. That is where real glory exists, and in that glory, we see freedom work by destroying what is corrupt within us. The power of the gospel makes us perfect and righteous before God.

Glory and Freedom Revealed

True freedom is remarkably desired among mankind. We know that we want it. We know that somewhere deep down in our souls, we haven't achieved it. Yet, we keep moving forward, like mindless lemmings striving for things we think will give us more freedom but actually enslave us more to corruption. Peter gives a hint of this: "They promise them freedom, but they themselves are slaves of corruption. For whatever overcomes a person, to that he is enslaved" (2 Pet. 2:19).

Again, a look at the world today proves everything I've just said. The world's population is only getting more corrupt.

Things aren't getting better. Everyone wants a solution that doesn't involve God. Mankind is devolving into evil at a rapid rate. But one group of people has discovered true freedom—the true believers.

I say "true believers" because a large majority of those who call themselves believers haven't fully committed their lives to God. If all professing believers fully committed their lives to God, the church wouldn't be shrinking in our world; it would be growing exponentially. True believers have experienced freedom. They have recognized that their status of glory has changed and is changing. These people are not neurotic. They aren't greedy jerks. They aren't overcome with malice or envy. They are not addicted to a lifestyle of sin. These people actually have found joy in life, and they are content. They understand that freedom does not happen in the flesh but in the spirit. They are perfectly content in life because of that revelation.

The tragedy of the mystery of freedom is that the whole world is longing for it, but they look everywhere except to those who have actually found it. This comes back to Solomon and the book of Ecclesiastes. The man who had everything still couldn't gain freedom from death. His only hope was to look to God as the righteous Judge. That is the hope of all who have found freedom in Christ. Fully commit your life to God, make yourself a slave to Him, and the opposite will happen. God will make you an heir in His family, and you will experience freedom and glory.

The Mystery of God-Breathed Scripture

All Scripture is breathed out by God and profitable for teaching, for reproof, for correction, and for training in righteousness (2 Tim. 3:16).

"No, it's just ink on a page," says the wise modern man. The Bible is just a book like any other book. It was written by fallible human authors. We are not to take the Bible literally. The Bible is full of inconsistencies. It was meant to teach a moral lesson, not depict real events. These are all comments I hear often, subtle, or not-so-subtle, ways to devalue the legitimacy of Scripture.

The truth is that the Bible is simply not like any other book written by man. As mentioned previously, it is the only ancient text in existence that was written by forty different authors over the span of 1,500 years, and yet the story is cohesive. It's not a mere book communicating a story for our potential benefit; rather it's a message of life spoken by God through human interaction. There is something about the Bible that is alive, and far beyond being alive in someone's imagination. The words themselves have a living quality to them.

Before Adam was being formed into the shape God wanted him to be, he was still just a clump of dust. He was an inanimate object with no true living qualities. However, when God breathed the breath of life into him, he became a living soul. He had life qualities where before there were none. In the same way, when Paul suggests that Scripture is a God-breathed thing, he is communicating that it has a life to it that no other writing in existence has. It is a direct reflection of Jesus Christ Himself, in the form of ink and paper.

There is a seriousness to this that cannot be denied. This is no ordinary book, and those who treat it as such have given up on the mystery that God has placed before us. The Word of God has power. It opens doors and tears down walls where nothing else will work. One of the prime examples we have of this is what Jesus Himself did when He was tempted by Satan in the wilderness:

> *Then Jesus was led up by the Spirit into the wilderness to be tempted by the devil. And after fasting forty days and forty nights, he was hungry. And the tempter came and said to him, "If you are the Son of God, command these stones to become loaves of bread."*
>
> *But he answered, "It is written, 'Man shall not live by bread alone, but by every word that comes from the mouth of God.'"*
>
> *Then the devil took him to the holy city and set him on the pinnacle of the temple and said to him, "If you are the Son of God, throw yourself down, for it is written, 'He will command his angels concerning you,' and 'On their hands they will bear you up, lest you strike your foot against a stone.'*
>
> *Jesus said to him, "Again it is written, 'You shall not put the Lord your God to the test.'"*
>
> *Again, the devil took him to a very high mountain and showed him all the kingdoms of the world and their glory. And he said to him, "All these I will give you, if you will fall down and worship me."*
>
> *Then Jesus said to him, "Be gone, Satan! For it is written, 'You shall worship the Lord your God and him only shall you serve'"* (Matt. 4:1–10).

Jesus was in a very real situation here. This wasn't happening in a dream. This wasn't some weird fantasy. He had been without food for forty days and nights. He was most likely in a sad physical state, and Satan put strong temptations in front of Him. The way Jesus responded should be telling to us. He quoted Scripture! He didn't call angels down. He didn't pray to God the Father for help. He quoted Scripture. He communicated a living truth. It was this truth that forced Satan to flee. Jesus' view of Scripture was that it was an ironclad message of truth. He quoted it often to the various people He encountered as a method of showing what was true and accurate. If Jesus didn't question the validity of Scripture, then why do we question it today?

The Battle over Inerrancy

Modern man, with his ever-growing intellectual prowess, simply cannot come to terms that ink on a page actually has power beyond the imagination or human determination. Therefore, a divinely inspired book cannot exist according to modern scholars. Thus, the Bible must be attacked and made illegitimate to the point of being like any other ancient faith text: good for contemplating and reflecting on but certainly not God-breathed words of truth.

In light of this, modern theological scholarship has jumped on a concept that has been poorly defined and misleading: inerrancy. By using the word inerrancy, this theology suggests that the entire Bible is without any sort of error in its original writings. Many believers claim to believe this. There is a small issue with this, though. The original written documents have not been discovered yet.

Houston, we have a problem! All we have are copies that have come down through the generations, compiled long after the originals were written. Much like the game of Telephone, after a while some copyist was bound to make a mistake here and there—and that is exactly what we see. Compounding this problem are the various translations of the Scriptures into different languages. Regardless of what anyone says, something is always lost in translation. So when we look at our English translation of what had been a Greek New Testament and a Hebrew/Aramaic Old Testament, we actually see the product of a group of translators' best efforts to transfer the story to us with the utmost accuracy possible.

Even with all this care, modern scholars say it is impossible for our modern Bibles to be without error, and I am perfectly fine agreeing with them. Having spent some extensive time and training in the original languages of the Scripture, I can see that our modern Bibles have thousands of variants. What is a variant? A variant is a difference from other copies of a manuscript. Usually these differences are something simple, like a copyist missed a punctuation mark or perhaps added a letter to the end of a word when it wasn't there before. We call these copyist errors, and they are often very easy to fix and do not affect the meaning of the text.

The translator will simply compare the majority of the copies that are in existence, and if the error is found in only one or two of them, they use what is found in the majority of the texts for their translation. Every once in a while, however, 50 percent of the texts may have a word written one way, and the other 50 percent have it written another way. At this point, the translators will simply make a judgment call. Even in those situations, most variants are still only punctuation or single letter mistakes, which have no effect on the meaning of the story.

However, there are a select few situations where whole phrases or sentences are in question. In English translations, these portions will be set in brackets. When we look through the Bible, we see that the number of instances of bracketed material could probably be counted on one or two hands. It is very little, and none of it truly affects the meaning of the story. For example, at the end of the Lord's Prayer in Matthew 6:13, a bracketed phrase says, "For thine is the Kingdom and the power and the glory forever, amen."

In some translations, this phrase isn't even included. Scholars do not know whether it should be there or not based upon the evidence of the copies. But the question must be asked: Whether the phrase is included or not, does it radically change the story? Does it alter the teaching? Not really! Plenty of Scripture passages allude to the same thing elsewhere. So, are there errors that actually alter the message and meaning of the story? Nope, not in any significant way.

But how can we be confident of this? The Bible has a bank of about 35,000 total copies, dating from recent history all the way back to within a generation of the original writings. It truly is an embarrassment of riches. The Bible by far has the most documented material to draw from. To put this into context, the other ancient writing that has the second most documented material is Homer's *Iliad*, which has approximately six hundred to a thousand copies in existence. So, the Bible has thirty-five times more evidence and material than the next most accurate ancient book. If we can't derive an accurate story from that much material, then we cannot trust any ancient document in existence.

Beyond all of this, it is important to note that the Old Testament writings were all completed by the time Jesus came on the scene. He quoted from them and treated them as authoritative. He even quoted from the Greek translations of the Old Testament as if they were still authoritative. If

God is doing that on earth, then we must have done something drastically wrong with our theology of inerrancy.

Whoever said that the Bible was a completely inerrant document in every single thing was foolish. The theology of inerrancy should say that the Bible is completely without error in the meaning of its message and the overall story. Wrong punctuation does not ruin an entire story. A copyist error does not ruin an entire story. To admit that there are errors within a written document does not delegitimize the message of the document.

The Results of Inerrancy

Inerrancy was the starting point, and it was used as a catchall "gotcha" statement for those who truly wanted to discredit the Bible. The more disturbing outcome of all of this was the slippery slope it created. All too quickly we went from questioning the minute details of Scripture to questioning the reality of some of the main content of Scripture.

The entire creation account in Genesis is now considered a battleground. Were Adam and Eve even real people? Did God really create the world in six days? Did all the people prior to the flood even exist? Did the flood even really take place? These questions are almost always rhetorical, an effort to chip away at the legitimacy of the story itself. And it's gone even further than that. Now some say Job probably wasn't a real person. Jonah probably never got swallowed by a real fish. Samson couldn't have really been that strong. All of these assertions are the product of the theology of inerrancy that has been grotesquely misused.

What started with inerrancy then turned to modern logic, which says that supernatural phenomena are simply not believable. Therefore, anything that seems fantastical probably didn't happen. Eventually, this method of questioning away truth will come back to Jesus. Did He really die on a cross and was He resurrected? Was He really born of a virgin? Did He even exist? At what point do those who say they believe in God have to draw the line before they realize that they really don't believe after all?

If God breathed into this story a living message of truth, then His credibility is on the line for its accuracy. Therefore, if people are really questioning the plotline of the story, they have gone beyond the human errors of translation and have attacked God directly. They are saying, through their rhetoric of skepticism, that God's story is not divine, not inspired, and certainly not accurate or beneficial beyond what the human intellect can do with it.

In other words, His Word lives and dies by human approval. For the world of nonbelievers, who cares? For the world of real believers, we know the truth, and we are confident in it. But for the world of believers who are caught up in the nonbelievers' logic, this is a very important line in the sand. Either you believe the story of Scripture, or you don't. There is no gray area here. This isn't an issue of believing in something that man has potentially corrupted. This is believing in something that God has validated Himself by His own breath.

The Power of a God-Breathed Word

The revealed mystery of a God-breathed Word is that it has real power. It's not just the power of influence among other people, but it has tangible power over real things. In Ephesians 6:17, Paul tells us to put on some armor, "and take the helmet of salvation, and the sword of the Spirit, which is the word of God." Notice that the Word of God is the sword of the Spirit. It's the only offensive weapon given to us. Everything else is used for defense.

The Word of God can be used in such a way that it does actual damage to things. It can also be used in such a way that it can greatly benefit others. Consider what Hebrews has to say:

> *For the word of God is living and active, sharper than any two-edged sword, piercing to the division of soul and of spirit, of joints and of marrow, and discerning the thoughts and intentions of the heart* (Heb. 4:12).

This is the power of the Word of God—the Scriptures—which again are reflective of an actual Person, Jesus Christ. Therefore, Christ in us means that the Word of God dwells in us. Truth is in us. The power of that truth is applied to us, and we can participate in it. But for those who deny God's validated truth, at the very least they will be left in the dark. It will be like holding a sword hilt with no blade attached to it. The mystery of a God-breathed Word is that it is the power of the children of God. How many believers today look at the Bible and simply don't see real power?

Truth Realized, Mysteries Revealed, and the Radical Gospel Working

None of what has been said in this chapter are mysteries to the intellect. Scripture has plainly told us what would happen if we would just follow its guidance and lead. If we fear the Lord, we know the results. If we commit to being a living sacrifice, we know what to expect. Glory and freedom are well explained, and the power of the Scripture is undeniable from a conceptual perspective. All of these things have been communicated!

But these are still true mysteries because the only way to fully understand them is to commit to God's parameters for them and then personally experience the results. God has been a genius in this, as He designed this process to be "faith first." No amount of training and intelligence will equate to an understanding of these mysteries. Only faith, only an experience with the Almighty God, will do.

The humble of heart come before God in fear and surrender their lives to Him fully, and they are the ones who will receive true knowledge and wisdom. The one who considers his physical life a sacrifice before God will experience living like never before. The one who has given glory to God and died to his physical life will really see freedom and enter into the glory of God. The one who has the Word of God dwelling within them, who fully believes in its truth, will have power.

This can be your reality today! God works in mysteries, and the Radical Gospel is a culmination of all of these manifesting in a person's life. I have experienced the amazing reality of these things and am continuing to experience it. They are more real to me than much of what I see with my own eyes in our tainted world. This is the pathway to abundant living. Life to the highest degree according to God's standard is afforded to those who truly believe. It is so very good that it is virtually indescribable. If only more people would take the leap and give everything they are to God, they would be changed forever.

12

Stand Firm and Endure in Obedience

God's promise of the ages is that He will start a Radical Gospel change in us right now, but He will not fully finish it until He returns. Therefore, this common theme runs throughout the whole New Testament. We are constantly affirmed to "stand firm" and/or "endure" until the end comes, and our salvation is fully completed. This is the real "perseverance of the saints."

In order to stand firm, we must know in what we are standing firm, and also against what we are standing firm. These Scriptures should shed some light on this:

Be watchful, stand firm in the faith, act like men, be strong (1 Corinthians 16:13).

Let all that you do be done in love (1 Corinthians 16:14).

Not that we lord it over your faith, but we work with you for your joy, for you stand firm in your faith (2 Corinthians 1:24).

Only let your manner of life be worthy of the gospel of Christ, so that whether I come and see you or am absent, I may hear of you that you are standing firm in one spirit, with one mind striving side by side for the faith of the gospel (Philippians 1:27).

Therefore, my brothers, whom I love and long for, my joy and crown, stand firm thus in the Lord, my beloved (Philippians 4:1).

So then, brothers, stand firm and hold to the traditions that you were taught by us, either by our spoken word or by our letter (2 Thessalonians 2:15).

Believers are all called to stand firm but in what? These verses tell us that we must stand firm in faith, in one unified spirit, in the Lord, and also in those traditions that have been taught by the apostolic leaders. Isn't it odd that God never said to stand firm in our 401k retirement plans? He never said that we should stand firm in our masterfully built homes or in our high-end luxury vehicles. He didn't even have the consideration to say that we should stand firm in our amazing job security.

God said to stand firm in faith. Faith is an affirmative response toward God, while reacting to truth. It is living out truth in our actions. We are to do this in the Spirit as one unified community of believers. We are to stand firm in our ever-increasing relationship with the Lord, and we are to stand firm in important traditional practices. These are all the mainstays of a solid believer in God. Likewise, all of these group together to form a one-word reality: obedience.

Stand Firm and Endure in Obedience

Our obedience to God is what keeps us from losing our footing. It helps us stay strong. It makes us persevere toward the end goal, which is our full redemption. But along the way, we are certainly not standing firm just to look statuesque. There is a purpose for this, and these Scriptures tell us why:

For freedom Christ has set us free; stand firm therefore, and do not submit again to a yoke of slavery (Galatians 5:1).

Therefore take up the whole armor of God, that you may be able to withstand in the evil day, and having done all, to stand firm (Ephesians 6:13).

We must stand firm so we don't become slaves once again! Slaves to what? Slaves to sin and death! We have freedom, remember, and freedom does not come without a battle. Therefore, Ephesians told us that we must stand firm in the midst of the evil days, when there is sure to be an attack from evil forces. All this rhetoric gives us the picture of maturity. A believer who has solidified his belief in truth through his actions becomes more and more firm in his footing. There is a verse for those who don't:

And he gave the apostles, the prophets, the evangelists, the shepherds and teachers, to equip the saints for the work of ministry, for building up the body of Christ, until we all attain to the unity of the faith and of the knowledge of the Son of God, to mature manhood, to the measure of the stature of the fullness of Christ, so that we may no longer be children, tossed to and fro by the waves and carried about by every wind of doctrine, by human cunning, by craftiness in deceitful schemes (Eph. 4:11–14).

If we don't grow in faith and learn to stand firm, there is a 100 percent probability that we will get knocked around by every wind of doctrine, human cunning, and deceitful schemes. This is a rather common occurrence in our world today, and sadly it often takes place within the church. Professing believers are getting knocked around in their faith all the time because they choose not to completely follow Jesus. They hold something back. They refrain from the practice of faith. They don't grow!

These believers are on very dangerous ground. In this case, there ought to be a real fear of falling away from the faith. Some people might ask if that is even possible. Others might say that when people fall away, they probably never really believed in the first place. However, we must consider what Scripture has to say:

> *For it is impossible, in the case of those who have once been enlightened, who have tasted the heavenly gift, and have shared in the Holy Spirit, and have tasted the goodness of the word of God and the powers of the age to come, and then have fallen away, to restore them again to repentance, since they are crucifying once again the Son of God to their own harm and holding him up to contempt* (Heb. 6:4–6).

This sobering passage truly seems to be depicting someone who has honestly entered into a relationship of faith with Jesus and then made the unbelievable decision to back out of that relationship and fully reject God. This is what we call "falling away," and its consequences are severe. As the writer of Hebrews says, it is impossible to restore such a person once again to repentance, since they will have crucified the Son of God again. How do you restore someone "again" to repentance unless they had already experienced real repentance and applied Jesus' sacrifice to their own life?

This is the difficult nature of a faith relationship with God, knowing that if we are not standing firm in a growing faith relationship with Him, then we are potentially in danger of the world convincing us to destroy that relationship. Jesus Himself doesn't have any more encouraging words in this regard, as He states:

> *Then they will deliver you up to tribulation and put you to death, and you will be hated by all nations for my name's sake. And then many will fall away and betray one another and hate one another. And many false prophets will arise and lead many astray. And because lawlessness will be increased, the love of many will grow cold. But the one who endures to the end will be saved* (Matt. 24:9–13).

There will be a great falling away of people from the faith. Our world will see people renouncing their faith en masse, and to some degree, this has already begun. Many so-called wise people, or prophets, will lead many astray. The love of many will grow cold because the laws are not good or not enforced, and evil will thrive. It sounds like a fairly good description of our world today. But the hope in all of this is for those who endure. The ones who endure to the end will be saved!

Endurance and standing firm go hand in hand. Standing firm has the connotation of someone holding his ground despite attack. Endurance more connotes someone running an arduous race. Our faith walk is a marathon, not a sprint. Those who enter into belief must not expect their faith experience to be a "once and done" act. It is a continuous work that builds and forms a person over his lifetime on earth. God repeatedly encourages us to endure and overcome:

> *Therefore, since we are surrounded by so great a cloud of witnesses, let us also lay aside every weight, and sin which clings so closely, and let us run with endurance the race that is set before us, looking to Jesus, the founder and perfecter of our faith, who for the joy that was set before him endured the cross, despising the shame, and is seated at the right hand of the throne of God. Consider him who endured from sinners such hostility against himself, so that you may not grow weary or fainthearted. In your struggle against sin you have not yet resisted to the point of shedding your blood. And have you forgotten the exhortation that addresses you as sons?*
>
> *My son, do not regard lightly the discipline of the Lord, nor be weary when reproved by him. For the Lord disciplines the one he loves, and chastises every son whom he receives. It is for discipline that you have to endure. God is treating you as sons. For what son is there whom his father does not discipline?* (Heb. 12:1–7)

This passage in Hebrews comes right after the chapter that highlights all those earlier believers who were regarded for their faith. Our encouragement to endure is partly based on being surrounded by "so great a cloud of witnesses." Yet these witnesses were far from perfect. Noah got drunk. Abraham pimped out his wife because he was scared that people would kill him over her beauty…and he did that more than once. Moses murdered an Egyptian and became a fugitive. Samson slept with prostitutes and often got drunk. David slept with another man's wife and then had that man killed on the battlefront to hide his lawlessness. Virtually every example of a person who had great faith was also an example of a person with great sins and flaws.

This should be a vast comfort to us, as our marathon of faith does not require perfection. Sin will still creep in here and there, but our true nature as believers is our dedication to turn once again back to God and allow Him to discipline us for our own good. The outcome of such discipline is that we will become more and more obedient to Him.

Obedience to God Is the Doorway to Growing Love

Standing firm and maintaining endurance has its roots in obedience. We are to stand firm upon the truth. We are to endure as God disciplines us into living out truth in our lives. In order to do these things, we must have a heart for obedience to God.

I've heard multiple times that Christianity is not a religion; it is a relationship. That seems like a true statement from a pop culture perspective, but in reality, what is being communicated is:

- Religion means following the rules and laws.
- Relationship means having a personal experience with God.

One is cold and heartless, and the other is warm and fuzzy. However, the truth is that religion involves man's attempt to reach out to God through various acts. It is part of a relationship. Likewise, a relationship with God relies on obedience to His commands. Following the rules and laws is part of a relationship with Him. Where the church has failed is that they have too often become the interpreter of God's commands, requiring things God never asked. Nevertheless, free expression is not something we see God promote in Scripture. Rather, He promotes godly expression:

As the Father has loved me, so have I loved you. Abide in my love. If you keep my commandments, you will abide in my love, just as I have kept my Father's commandments and abide in his love. These things I have spoken to you, that my joy may be in you, and that your joy may be full (John 15:9–11)

We are called to abide in Jesus' love—not in our own determination of what love is, but in the love that He reveals to us. What does that love look like? It looks like obedience. There is no more plain and simple Scripture in the Bible in regard to growing in love. If we learn and follow Jesus' commands, then we will understand love more and more each and every day.

This love is the life source of a relationship with God. Without this growing love, people will be more susceptible to falling away from the faith. Without love, every other part of a faith walk simply won't make much sense. It won't work. Paul has some important insight into this:

If I speak in the tongues of men and of angels, but have not love, I am a noisy gong or a clanging cymbal. And if I have prophetic powers, and understand all mysteries and all knowledge, and if I have all faith, so as to remove mountains, but have not love, I am nothing. If I give away all I have, and if I deliver up my body to be burned, but have not love, I gain nothing (1 Cor. 13:1–3).

Paul suggests that even if we have every other component of faith, including a full understanding of all of the mysteries of God, all the knowledge necessary for faith, and the gifts of God in abundance, if love is not part of this equation, then there is zero value in our efforts. We have absolutely no capacity for growth without love being the center of growth within us. And the only way that this love will develop is through trusting obedience to Jesus and His commands. This is an inconvenient truth to many people because few of us want love to be the result of following a bunch of rules, even the rules of Jesus. We want love to be the abstract and uplifting feeling that comes from relational interaction and feeling close. If we really want that closeness, however, the rules and commands come first. That's the way the cookie crumbles.

Those Who Overcome, and Those Who Fall Away

For those people who cannot come to terms with a love that grows within them out of the obedience to Christ that they live out, there is a clear conclusion. We find this in one of Jesus' parables:

> *Enter by the narrow gate. For the gate is wide and the way is easy that leads to destruction, and those who enter by it are many. For the gate is narrow and the way is hard that leads to life, and those who find it are few.... Not everyone who says to me, "Lord, Lord," will enter the kingdom of heaven, but the one who does the will of my Father who is in heaven. On that day many will say to me, "Lord, Lord, did we not prophesy in your name, and cast out demons in your name, and do many mighty works in your name?" And then will I declare to them, "I never knew you; depart from me, you workers of lawlessness"* (Matt. 7:13–23).

Jesus Himself depicts the way of true life to be a narrow gate that few people actually find. Wide is the path to destruction, and according to this, many who believe they are doing things for God and living a good, clean life will not enter the kingdom of heaven. It is not enough to merely perform outward expressions of righteousness. We must also be internally changed, transformed, and growing in love.

The people who live devoid of real love in their lives will be the ones who finally see Jesus on Judgment Day and plead their case to Him, but He will declare, "I never knew you, depart from Me, you workers of lawlessness." Do you see the process here? Jesus says that if we follow His commands, then we will abide in His love. If we are not abiding and growing in Jesus' love, then that is evidence we have not followed His commands.

Therefore, whether or not those people seem to be doing good things for God, it is still lawlessness because they never followed the commands of God. It is these people who are on

Stand Firm and Endure in Obedience

the wiry edge of falling away, and Scripture describes the various pits into which they are likely to fall:

> *For the time is coming when people will not endure sound teaching, but having itching ears they will accumulate for themselves teachers to suit their own passions, and will turn away from listening to the truth and wander off into myths* (2 Tim. 4:3–4).

> *I say this in order that no one may delude you with plausible arguments. For though I am absent in body, yet I am with you in spirit, rejoicing to see your good order and the firmness of your faith in Christ. Therefore, as you received Christ Jesus the Lord, so walk in him, rooted and built up in him and established in the faith, just as you were taught, abounding in thanksgiving. See to it that no one takes you captive by philosophy and empty deceit, according to human tradition, according to the elemental spirits of the world, and not according to Christ* (Col. 2:4–8)

I could not script out a more accurate analysis of our day. Those who are not built up in Christ and firmly rooted in a love relationship with Him, which is growing through their faith walk, are targets for captivity through vain philosophies, empty deceits, and even human traditions that all lead away from Christ. Once people are sufficiently duped by these things, they will not put up with sound doctrine derived from truth any longer. Rather, in their pride, they will find many experts and teachers who agree with their own bias and use that as justification to wander away from God but still claim that they are doing the will of God.

Falling away happens—and it can happen to anyone. It has happened to people whom the masses thought were extremely strong believers in God. Jesus warned us to be prepared as it was going to happen on a massive scale within the church. The only way to combat such a thing is to return to Scripture.

The reintroduction to truth is the only real antidote for those who are in the process of falling away, but who haven't quite finished their rejection of God. The best passage of Scripture to point out people who are in this state is John 15. This is a great introduction to the basics of faith for any believer, but John wrote it with one goal in mind. In John 16:1, he says, "I have said all these things to you to keep you from falling away."

It is John's desire not to see people go down the road of falling away, and his prescription to prevent this was paring down everything to simple terms. It's just you and Christ, and a relationship with Him that is growing will look a certain way. It's as simple as that.

On the other end of the spectrum, we have the overcomers, those people who entered by the narrow gate, who kept a firm stance and endured in their faith walk with God, growing in love each and every day. It's these people who will fulfill their salvation when Christ comes again. At that time, an inheritance is waiting for them. Who knows all the things God has in store for believers once the redemption is fully completed? Yet we do have a glimpse of some of the things that will be inherited:

Stand Firm and Endure in Obedience

He who has an ear, let him hear what the Spirit says to the churches. To the one who conquers I will grant to eat of the tree of life, which is in the paradise of God (Revelation 2:7).

He who has an ear, let him hear what the Spirit says to the churches. The one who conquers will not be hurt by the second death (Revelation 2:11).

He who has an ear, let him hear what the Spirit says to the churches. To the one who conquers I will give some of the hidden manna, and I will give him a white stone, with a new name written on the stone that no one knows except the one who receives it (Revelation 2:17).

The one who conquers and who keeps my works until the end, to him I will give authority over the nations, and he will rule them with a rod of iron, as when earthen pots are broken in pieces, even as I myself have received authority from my Father (Revelation 2:26–27).

The one who conquers will be clothed thus in white garments, and I will never blot his name out of the book of life. I will confess his name before my Father and before his angels (Revelation 3:5).

The one who conquers, I will make him a pillar in the temple of my God. Never shall he go out of it, and I will write on him the name of my God, and the name of the city of my God, the new Jerusalem, which comes down from my God out of heaven, and my own new name (Revelation 3:12).

The one who conquers, I will grant him to sit with me on my throne, as I also conquered and sat down with my Father on his throne (Revelation 3:21).

These references are from the messages that Christ sent to the seven churches at the beginning of the book of Revelation. The word "conquers" in each of these is the same Greek word as is used for "overcomes." Therefore, the one who overcomes will receive rewards at the end of the road. Just think about that: The overcomers will eat of the tree of life in the paradise of God, and they will sit on the throne next to Jesus. They will rule over the nations with Christ. They will be given a new name, specifically picked out by God Himself. Jesus will confess their names before the Father and the angels. Furthermore, they will have a permanent place within the temple of God. Finally, there is the promise that they will not have to experience the second death, which is judgment in hell.

This is what believers are fighting for! This is what the patient endurance of the faithful will be rewarded with. The goal of the Radical Gospel is that when the race is finished and the gospel has been completed, those who remain will have this inheritance. From my perspective, these things are worth fighting for. These things are worth standing firm in the faith, enduring the discipline of the Lord, and living a life of obedience to Him.

Which path are you on? The wide gate, caught up in the world, surrounding yourself with people who agree with you? Or do you have a holy discontent until you reach that narrow gate, unwavering in faith, growing in love, and standing firm in the truth that God has presented? For some, this may be a tough choice. For me, my choice was easy.

13

A Proverbial Future

This may sound like an over-the-top cliché, but this entire book comes down to one key insight: trust God. How much are you willing to trust Him? The proverb I engraved on my walking stick, which has brought me through some of the most difficult times of my life, states:

Trust in the Lord with all your heart and lean not on your own understanding. In all your ways acknowledge him and he will make your paths straight (Prov. 3:5–6).

I look to each new day with these words in mind. Everything I think I know takes a back seat to my trust in the Lord. I rely on Him with every fiber of my being. I seek to have a better relationship with Him each and every day, and I have full assurance that He will make my life path for each day clear and walkable. If this is what my future looks like for the rest of the days of my life and on into eternity, I am perfectly happy living such a life.

Our main problem was that we all will die, so we might as well "eat, drink, and be merry." But the proverbial reality is that God has defeated death, and He will walk each of us through the darkest of places. It is a constant choice we must make throughout each and every day: trust God or don't trust God. What's your choice?

The Radical Gospel Is Not for the Faint-Hearted

You have to be tough to experience the full-fledged gospel in your life. It is not an easy process to fall into the hands of the living God and have Him turn your world upside down, destroying your old life and building a brand-new one. It can be painful, it can be scary, and it can cause you to feel like you've almost lost who you are. It certainly isn't about coffee sipping, Scripture debating, a laser-light show with smoke machines, singing pop worship songs that don't make sense, or feel-good prosperity talk about how God's plans for you will lead to pleasant living. The gospel is raw. It's real! It's in your face. That's the way God does it.

You can't build something new until the old has been fully ripped apart and discarded. You will not get to peace and joy until God deals with the ugly parts of your life: the abuse, the divorces, the scandals, the lying, the cheating, the depression, the anxiety, and ultimately the sin within you. God is going to grab all of that and rip it out of your life. It is going to hurt badly, but it is necessary. Do you trust Him?

It is not until you reach this point that the mysteries of God will truly be revealed in your life: the knowledge and wisdom from fearing Him, the life-giving truth of being a living sacrifice, the release from all the bondage holding you down, and the newly discovered power in the God-breathed Word of Truth. All of these will begin to make more and more sense as God continues to work in your life, but you must approach them in faith and potentially look the fool to the rest of the world. Do you trust Him?

Don't forget that the God who is offering this Radical

Gospel is a loving Creator but also a righteous Judge. He wants to make a way for every person to choose Him, but He is not afraid to judge those who do not. He is purely righteous and lovingly merciful. His grace has an end, but His love does not. Are you willing to trust in who He is?

True joy and true peace are a result of this gospel doing its work in your life. Some may think that they are perfectly joyful and peaceful already; therefore, they either live the gospel or they don't need the gospel. For those people, I have a few questions. Do you have peace and joy at the thought of your own physical death? How about the death of your children? The peace that surpasses all understanding exists even in the midst of these events. Unspeakable joy can ring true despite death. Is that the case with you? Do you trust God to actually bring that about in your life? What are you going to do?

The Never-Ending Mystery of God's Love within You

Once again, everything comes back around to this thing called love. Of all the knowledge and wisdom and mysteries of God that are discovered within the Scriptures and promised to the one who believes, love is the one thing that may never be fully discovered in this life or the next. God's nature is our pursuit. As we learn about Him and come to know Him, we will learn about love and begin to know love. This learning process may just last into the ages of eternity.

To trust in God is to allow yourself to be vulnerable enough for Him to show the innermost "you" what love really is. Do you want that level of transparency? The love of God within you will be the most intrusive force in your life. There will be no separation, no safe space, and no reprieve from what His love will do. Do you trust Him with that?

The masses seem to wish for people to simply love each other. They also want to be loved. Yet I believe they have a terribly small and feeble view of love. If all you want in life is to be cared for, shown affection, served, prioritized, and treated with respect and dignity, I've got news for you—you have an impotent view of love. This love is focused primarily upon the fallen human person and not on the Spirit of God. It's not that those things are bad by any means, but if your body is going to cease to function at some point, why waste your loving efforts on only that?

God seeks to give you a relational experience beyond the physical fallen person. The love of God involves an intertwined and fused spirit with His Spirit. It involves a conjoined disposition and personality. That means what God thinks and feels, you will think and feel. What He is passionate about, you will be passionate about. However you are affected by things, He will share in at the most personal of levels. What moves God's heart will be moving to your heart. His love within you is the power source of any kind of change. Paul was adamant in saying that without love, even if you have everything else, in reality you have nothing.

The love of God in each individual certainly has common traits with all human beings, but it also has qualities unique to each individual. Therefore, the love of God is a one-of-a-kind experience for each person. Only you can experience the love of God within you. No one else can have your experience. Thus, if you reject God and His love, you will give up the most unique thing you will ever experience in your life. The stakes don't get any higher.

Yet, the sinful world will do everything it can to make love appear usual and ordinary; initially exciting, yet common. Everyone wants it, but once they have it, it becomes blissful and eventually boring. For example, people who have great marriages and good families do stupid things like have affairs. It's why people are never content with what they have, but they always seem to want something more or something different. It's why love in this world is almost always depicted in the finiteness of a physical or emotional experience.

In a world of sin, love can certainly not be something that is exciting forevermore. It must eventually become mundane because sin will be the thing that looks the most exciting. That is how the world prevents people from growing in God. They become blinded to real love, and they are left thoroughly discontented with the pseudo-love they experience.

God has the most mind-bending, life-altering relational experience for you that will never end, but He requires a whole life commitment to Him. Is the outcome worth the cost for you? Do you want ever-abundant life?

The Abundant Life

This God-promised abundant life starts at the point of belief and ends at the crossroads of never. Those things promised prior to our resurrection include a new spiritual creation birthed within us, peace, joy, understanding, provision—and the list goes on. Upon our resurrection, God has promised us a new immortal physical body; a brand-new name; cost-free food; a dwelling place in heaven; riches and rewards based upon the works we accomplished in serving Him on earth; a job ruling the nations with Christ; and ultimately, unhindered access to and a relationship with God Himself.

This is what we call hope. It's what we expect to happen, but it hasn't happened yet. Therefore, we eagerly await the fulness of life upon our resurrection with anticipation. This is the draw that helps us continue to live our current lives surrounded by corruption. The Bible consistently falls back on hope as a driving force:

> *Therefore, preparing your minds for action, and being sober-minded, set your hope fully on the grace that will be brought to you at the revelation of Jesus Christ* (1 Pet. 1:13)

> *I do not cease to give thanks for you, remembering you in my prayers, that the God of our Lord Jesus Christ, the Father of glory, may give you the Spirit of wisdom and of revelation in the knowledge of him, having the eyes of your hearts enlightened, that you may know what is the hope to which he has called you, what are the riches of his glorious inheritance in the saints* (Eph. 1:16–18).

Abundant living is accepting the type of life God has ordained for each and every one of us. It is a life filled with an inheritance, a future, and zero corruption. Anything less than this is not the type of living we were designed to experience. What type of life do you want? It is all too easy to only focus on life in the here and now, but wisdom would say that we ought to plan for our future. What do you want your future to look like? A lavish lifestyle now and hell later? Or perhaps a servant-minded and obedient lifestyle now and later royal living for eternity?

Hope must be fixed on the life we truly want or we will surely settle for something far less than we can attain. The abundant life is within our grasp; all we must do to achieve it is develop our belief in Christ by responding to His truth with our faith. We will then experience the grace of God that will accomplish this abundant life in us and through us.

A Word to Nonbelievers

If you are not a believer and have made it all the way through the book to this point, I commend your tenacity to read through things with which you don't agree. I hope my words and life experiences with God have at least caused some interest for change within your life.

If not, then I want you to know that I sincerely hope you find the fun and excitement in life that this world has to offer. I would certainly think that the whole "eat, drink, and be merry" lifestyle can accomplish some of that. Find a career that makes plenty of money, move to Portland, Oregon—the foodie capital of the country—and have a blast.

On the other hand, if you have had a change within, find a church. Find someone who has experienced the gospel in their life. Read through John 15, then read the book of Romans, and give it a fair shot. You might just find that committing to God will be worth it in the end. That was my experience. If you start, don't give up. Faith takes tenacity and stubbornness. Get ready for God to rock your world!

A Word to Those on the Wiry Edge of Belief

Seek God out! Don't give up on what God has provided

for you! If you find yourself weighed down by sin and the pain of this world, don't throw in the towel. Give 100 percent of who you are to God and see what happens. Don't hold anything back.

If you are having trouble believing in something that doesn't make sense to your human mind, just look at the world. A lot of what we see doesn't make any sense. You might as well give God's plan an honest try. But you must make a definitive choice—none of this wishy-washy stuff. Either you choose God, or you don't. Then go with it.

I was one of you all throughout my childhood and teenage years. If my experience means anything to you, it would be so much better if you leapt into the hands of God and didn't look back. It is totally worth it!

A Word from Me to You

I am not a judge. I am not an expert from any worldly standard. I am just a humble follower of Jesus who has experienced a large amount of hell on earth. I have walked through low points with Him and have been better for it. My real-world experience with God has been my guide for everything I have written in this book. Although I have been very critical of intellectualism and logic throughout this writing, I must say that I am not at all against such pursuits.

I believe that training and education are very valuable tools to help us learn how to think. I myself have devoted a large portion of my life to being trained in things relating to the Bible. However, intellectual thought is no substitute for a relational experience with God, just like a Facebook relationship is no substitute for a face-to-face relationship. If I were to accomplish anything with this writing, my hope would be that people might become more willing to lay aside their intellectual dogmas for a time and seek out the Person of God.

When I turned to the Person of God, I discovered Someone who would walk with me. He has cried with me. He has mourned with me. He has produced a supernatural rest for me. He has smacked me over the head like a loving Father would. He has gone ahead of me and opened doors in my path. He has laughed with me. He has given me dreams about my kids. He has worked within me, and He has also made me work within myself. He has been blessed by my worship of Him. Yet He has been grieved by me. He has been disappointed with me. He has had to extend grace far beyond what He should have had to extend. He's pulled me out of the muck and the mire more than once. He's not afraid to see the ugly parts in me. He teaches me about love every day. He has provided my basic needs. He has produced joy within my spirit. He has allowed trials and hardships in my life. He has helped to break the hold of anxiety and depression on me. He stood with me for four years while I was ill. He was not absent from me when I had to bury my children. For fifteen years of following Jesus in my life, not once was He unfaithful to the things He promised. Rather, He did far more than He promised He would. This is the God I have come to know.

If I, having come to know this amazing God, suppressed my experience with Him from the rest of the world, I would be no better than the most vile of dictators, the most heartless of serial killers, or the most corrupt of politicians. I would be instigating the beginning of sin, the suppression of truth. None of what I have said has been with the intention to judge, cast blame, make people feel guilty, or anything of that matter.

My true desire is that my testimony and experience would be a view of God some have never seen but desperately wished they had. I hate seeing people suffer. I hate seeing what sin and evil produces in people. I strongly desire to see people choose God and witness what God can do! It is my God-given calling to present the truth to people, the gospel of Jesus Christ. This is the best way I know to do that.

A Final Word

The most precious gift that you have in this world is the ability to choose how you wish to live your life. Sometimes much of that choice is taken away through various circumstances. Yet there is one choice that absolutely nothing and no one can take away from you. Your choice to believe is entirely yours! What is the most valuable thing in which you can believe?

If it doesn't solve the problem of death, may I suggest that it is not valuable enough. If you have become content with the idea that there is nothing after death, is that a belief that makes sense to your uniqueness in creation? Are you really just a flash in the pan? All these thoughts come from a feigned spirituality. There is only one belief that I have found that upholds value, deals with sin and death, and actually holds a future for humanity. It explains pain and helps us to live in joy. It is built on truth and reality. It provides the only way to change our lives from the inside out and lets us live on into the ages of eternity. It is the Radical Gospel of Jesus Christ.

About the Author

JAYSON DEROWITSCH has been involved in many forms of ministry throughout his life. He's done missions work overseas, homeless ministry, youth work, and is now residing as the Senior Pastor at Columbia View Church in Eastern Oregon.

Having a Master's degree in Theology, his training and work have been a testament to his relationship with God, and his experience with the Gospel. He enjoys living a blessed life with his wife, Stephanie, and son, Cyrus, as they always find new adventures in the high desert of Oregon.

To contact the author and to request speaking engagements: https://www.facebook.com/jaysonderowitsch

www.ingramcontent.com/pod-product-compliance
Lightning Source LLC
Chambersburg PA
CBHW030150100526
44592CB00009B/208